Nate Lowman: Before and After

Aspen Art Museum

Jim Lewis
Heidi Zuckerman

Nate Lowman: Before and After
Aspen Art Museum

Nate Lowman: Before and After
Aspen Art Museum

Contents

Foreword

It is the Aspen Art Museum's great pleasure to present this
publication on Nate Lowman's work in conjunction with his solo
exhibition at the museum, *Before and After*. Featuring Lowman's
painting production from 2004 to present, the exhibition in
Galleries 2 & 3 highlighted the concepts of desire and longing
so palpable within his practice. As a selective grouping, his
canvases were both light and heavily dark, the latter often
leaving visitors with a sense of melancholia. Most of Lowman's
subjects are determined by his own experiences and, likewise,
our museumgoers brought their own subjectivities to Lowman's
canvases filled with celebrities, news stories, smiley faces,
and other ephemera defining contemporary American culture.
This publication reflects and expands upon the ideas explored
within the galleries.

Of course, we are ever grateful to the numerous lenders to
this exhibition, including: Sascha S. Bauer; the Brant Foundation,
Greenwich, CT; Cromwell Art, LLC; David Zwirner, New York/
London/Hong Kong; the Dicke Collection; Susan and Leonard
Feinstein; Leo Fitzpatrick; Mark Fletcher and Tobias Meyer; Larry
Gagosian; the Ganek Family Foundation; Jeanne Greenberg
Rohatyn and Jackie Greenberg; Maccarone, New York/Los Angeles;
Massimo De Carlo, Milano/London/Hong Kong; Mugrabi
Collection; Rubell Family Collection, Miami; David Simkins;
Monica and Richard Weinberg; and several private collections.

For his contribution to this book, I would like to thank Jim
Lewis for his text, "The Hang and How to Think of It." It was
a pleasure hosting Lewis as our 2017 Writer in Residence, which
allowed him to visit Aspen and spend time with the exhibition.
As a result, his essay highlights a significant facet of Lowman's
practice and approach to working in a space. Special thanks are
due to Michele Maccarone of Maccarone gallery for her support
throughout the organization of the exhibition. My gratitude is also
extended to Camille Beinhorn, Lowman's studio manager, who
assisted with making arrangements and provided countless images
of the artist's archive during our research and the production of
this catalogue.

Additional thanks should be given to our staff at the Aspen
Art Museum. For their work on this publication, I am appreciative
of the risk-taking vision of and execution by David Wise, Graphic
Designer; Adjunct Editor Sarah Stephenson, who closely worked
on Lewis's contribution as well as the interview between Lowman
and myself; and former Curatorial Associate and Rights &
Reproduction Manager, Lauren Fulton, who collected images for
the catalogue and worked with me to develop *Before and After*.

Furthermore, for their work on Lowman's exhibition, I
want to thank Courtenay Finn, former Senior Curator; Jonathan
Hagman, Installation Director, and our remarkable team of
preparators; Luis Yllanes, Chief Operating Officer; and Jackie
Zorn, former Registrar.

Of course, I could never forget to mention the incredible
support of Susan and Larry Marx and their endowment for all of
our exhibitions. Additionally, generous support for Lowman's
show was provided by Erin Leider-Pariser and Paul Pariser, as well

as Rona and Jeffrey Citrin. Thanks also go to Toby Devan Lewis
for her endowment of our publications fund. I also want to thank the
AAM National Council for its continued financial assistance.
One hundred percent of its contributions go to directly support our
ambitious exhibitions.

Finally, I would like to thank Nate Lowman for his thoughtful
approach to working with our staff at the AAM to produce an
exhibition that was a favorite amongst visitors. His generosity in
sharing his archive was incredibly helpful and necessary for
arriving at a presentation that gives a clear but pointed look at the
breadth of Lowman's practice and its uncanny oscillation between
the personal and universal.

Heidi Zuckerman
Nancy and Bob Magoon CEO and Director

The Hang and How to Think of It
Jim Lewis

At dinner the night before this show opened in Aspen, I mentioned
to Nate Lowman a hypothesis I've been mulling over for the past
few months. The essential unit of aesthetic apprehension is not,
I'm starting to think, the individual painting or sculpture: it's the
exhibition. That is, no single work can be understood outside
the context of the artist's other works. It can barely be seen—seen
for what it is, I mean.

Take, for example, Robert Ryman—an extreme case, perhaps,
but not different in kind from all the others. Were I to walk into
someone's house with a Ryman on the wall, I'd scarcely notice
it unless it was pointed out to me, and I'm a great admirer of the
man. More to the point, put me in a museum with a Ryman
on the wall and a companion who knows little about these things,
and I'd find it difficult to explain what was extraordinary about it;
and even if I could, I doubt I would be convincing. But give
me a room full of Rymans and I'd scarcely need to say a word.
A bit of white on a single board is hard to hold on to. A few dozen
grouped together is almost unspeakably beautiful.

The same phenomenon plays out, in a more subtle way, with
individual gallery shows. The only way to get a good fix on a
new painting by, say, Brice Marden is to see it alongside the other
works he was making at the same time, and, thereafter, it will
be associated, consciously or unconsciously, with the body of work
within which it originally appeared.

The show's the thing. All artists are, to one degree or another,
installation artists. At dinner that night, I took this idea as far
as I could, suggesting that there's no such thing as a masterpiece,
because there's barely such a thing as an individual painting.
Lowman shook his head; he was skeptical, at best, which is
understandable but also curious, because no artist I can think of
is better at hanging a show than he is. So while I could happily
talk about the individual paintings herein, and say fine things about
them, I want to talk about the show—about the hang—instead.

By "the hang," I mean what goes where, what order the
paintings take, how high up the wall they're placed, how much space
there is between them. I also mean sightlines and sense-memory,
what you see when you turn around, what lies on the other side of the
wall, in the next room. I mean echoes from one painting to another,
rhymes and dissonances; I mean what's enough and what's too
much. I mean the height of the ceiling, traffic flow, the color of the
walls, the lighting (I've had long talks with artists about lightbulbs),
what gets reflected in windows, what's framed or unframed,
labeled or unlabeled, paired up or alone.

It's a sidelong and often overlooked talent, hanging a bunch
of paintings on a wall, and often a matter of instinct more than
intellect—a somewhat occult skill, hard to explain, like knowing
when a chord is in or out of tune. Artists love to talk about it,
and it's often the first thing you hear when you ask how a show
was: the work was great, but the hang was all wrong, the paintings
were too high, or too low, or the whole didn't cohere in some
important way; or, conversely, the hang was brilliant and made
the work look that much better. But art schools, so far as I know,
don't teach it, and critics rarely mention it. Lowman, as I say,
is especially good at it. I hope that my descriptions here will start
to explain why.

There are two rooms. One is large, airy, bright, and busy, with several doors leading in from the museum's lobby, and floor-to-ceiling windows that look out onto the street. The other is considerably smaller, quieter, windowless, and accessible only through a single door that leads from the first. In the first room, there are roughly forty works—predominantly, though not entirely, images of women, most of whom, though not all of whom, are famous. At least four of them are multiplied: two pictures, stacked on top of each other, of Julia Roberts (page 20); two renditions of plastic surgery sitting side by side on a wall above the windows (page 32); three of Lowman's versions of de Kooning's painting of Marilyn Monroe; and two versions of a picture of Nicole Brown Simpson, separated by a good twenty feet or so, and with two paintings in between (page 19). The rest range from the Venus of Willendorf to movie stars to anonymous girls and women.

The second room is considerably more intimate and contains about half as many works, arrayed on the walls of an elongated but high-ceilinged space. It feels like a chapel, in part because of its dimensions and in part because Lowman plays on them: one end is dominated by a shaped canvas containing a well-known portrait of the martyred Terri Schiavo, which sits next to another large painting overlaid with AA bumper stickers and printed with a few texts, one of them announcing "Keep the Faith" (page 29). On the opposite wall, there are angels and flowers (page 26). This is not, I should say, the first time he's used degraded Christian imagery to define a space, either ironically or for real—his show at the Brant Foundation a few years ago included a range of pickup truck drive trains rising up from the floor, crucifix-style, so that the gallery felt like a churchyard cemetery. I should also point out that Lowman denies having any such intention, though I can't say I really care. Content follows cadence: if you write a blues song in 6/8, it's going to sound like gospel, even if the lyrics are about Saturday night.

Sixty paintings are a lot for a space this size. A standard show by another artist in roughly equivalent rooms might contain fifteen or twenty. But Lowman tends to hang in a kind of drunken salon style, the paintings stacked hectically and off plumb, and this, too, is part of what gives the show an air of installation art, since it doesn't conduce to look at the paintings one by one (though it doesn't make it impossible, either). The angels and flowers, for example, are individual works, but arranged together as they are— in a diamond pattern smack in the center of the wall—they might just as easily be one. And their position opposite Schiavo binds the whole space together, giving it a single tone: both unnerving and irreverent, like a horror movie from the nineties.

Let's go back to the first room. It's considerably more worldly, more informed by the media, more focused on photography. Of the twenty or so works on the rear wall, for example, only two small ones are of men alone, and four or five more of men or boys playing ancillary roles to women (page 21). Eight are of women alone, and this pattern gets repeated, somewhat less dramatically, around the room: Joan Rivers, Jane Fonda, and Julia Roberts. Scarlett Johansson with a couple of soldiers (page 22). From outside the museum, looking through the wide glass wall, you see an array of female figures, almost all beautiful, healthy, primped, and

sleek, in significant contrast to Schiavo in the other gallery. Still, the
tagline attached to the ice cream cones in two of the paintings—
"I'll be dead soon"—appears in this room, not the other, and seems
to apply, not so much to Schiavo, as to the women here who soon
passed away: Nicole Brown Simpson, Marilyn Monroe, and
Joan Rivers. There is a certain morbidity beneath the gloss: in the
midst of life, we are in death.

It's notable that many of these pictures are in black-and-
white, like a tabloid from the days when death was rendered in
duotone; and even some of the color ones are overlaid with
the kind of broken black lines one would see in a Xerox of a Xerox.
That gives Lowman another rhythm to explore, and the beats
of color are carefully controlled. One of the black-and-white Julia
Roberts paintings, for example, is stacked on top of the other,
though they're distinct works; but the three Marilyns are put on two
separate walls, some distance apart—as they have to be, since
they're the brightest paintings of the lot. Color like that must be
parceled out, and, in fact, rarely are two color paintings, of any
sort, hung side by side. To do so would draw the eye too violently
and throw the entire exhibition off balance.

Much the same is true of the integrity of the paintings
themselves—that is, the degree to which the images on them are
either clear and legible or degraded, blurry, hard-to-make-out.
Like the colors, this comes and goes, in and out of focus, and Lowman
modulates through the stages subtly: low-res images cushioning
sharp ones; sharp ones placed so as not to overpower the more
degraded ones. The shift from one to the other becomes a rhythm,
as regular as breathing, your eyes squinting and relaxing as you
pass from one to the next.

You are breathing, the exhibition is breathing, you're
looking at the paintings and they're looking at you, watching you
as you pass before them. You turn and find that others have
been watching you from behind, though some are gazing off at
an angle, and one or two more are walking away. You could draw
sightlines that would dart around the galleries like one of those
laser security systems you see in movies, a web of gazes, including
your own. And this, too, is an element of the hang, perhaps
the most complex one, and the one most reliant on instinct. We are
contemplating a show composed primarily of portraits, which
is just to say that you're spending most of your time either looking
at someone else's eyes, or looking for them. They are trying to
get your attention. You are trying to get theirs.

A successful hang is attention's handmaiden: it directs your
focus, your notice, your consideration. So Lowman is guiding
your attention to attention itself, nudging your gaze as it settles on
one portrait and then moves on to the next, providing moments
of focus followed by moments of respite, certainty followed by
obscurity, pleasure interspersed with dismay, comfort with
foreboding, eye contact with disguise. I've suggested above that
this is a kind of rhythm, a beat, loose but not lawless, which steers
viewers around the galleries and governs their experience. It is
no trivial matter, no afterthought or rote exercise: it is an art unto
itself, demanding, expressive, rich, and, above all, powerful.
You will know more for knowing it, and see more by its guidance.
As Charles Olson once said, "He who controls rhythm, controls."

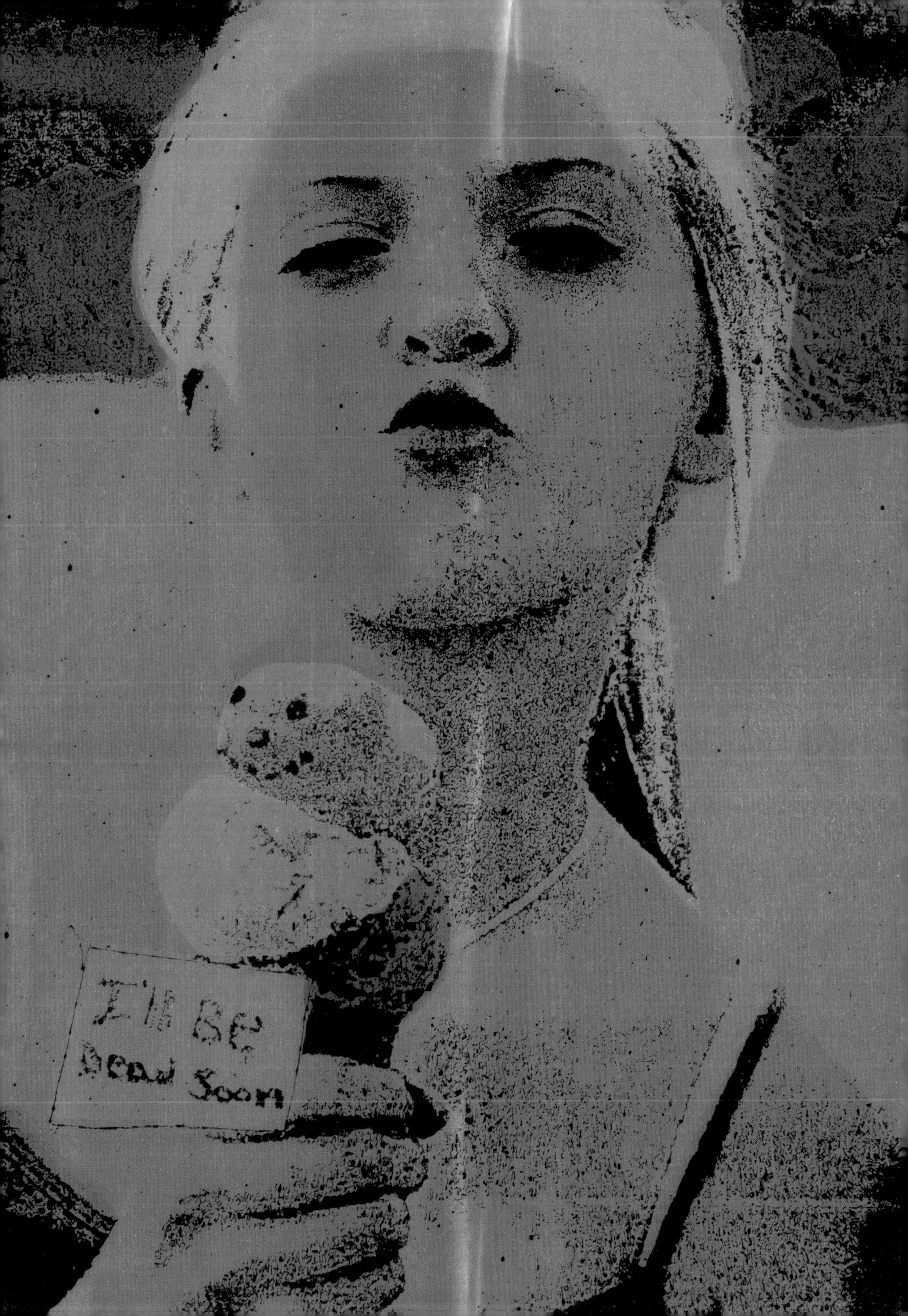
I'll Be
Dead Soon

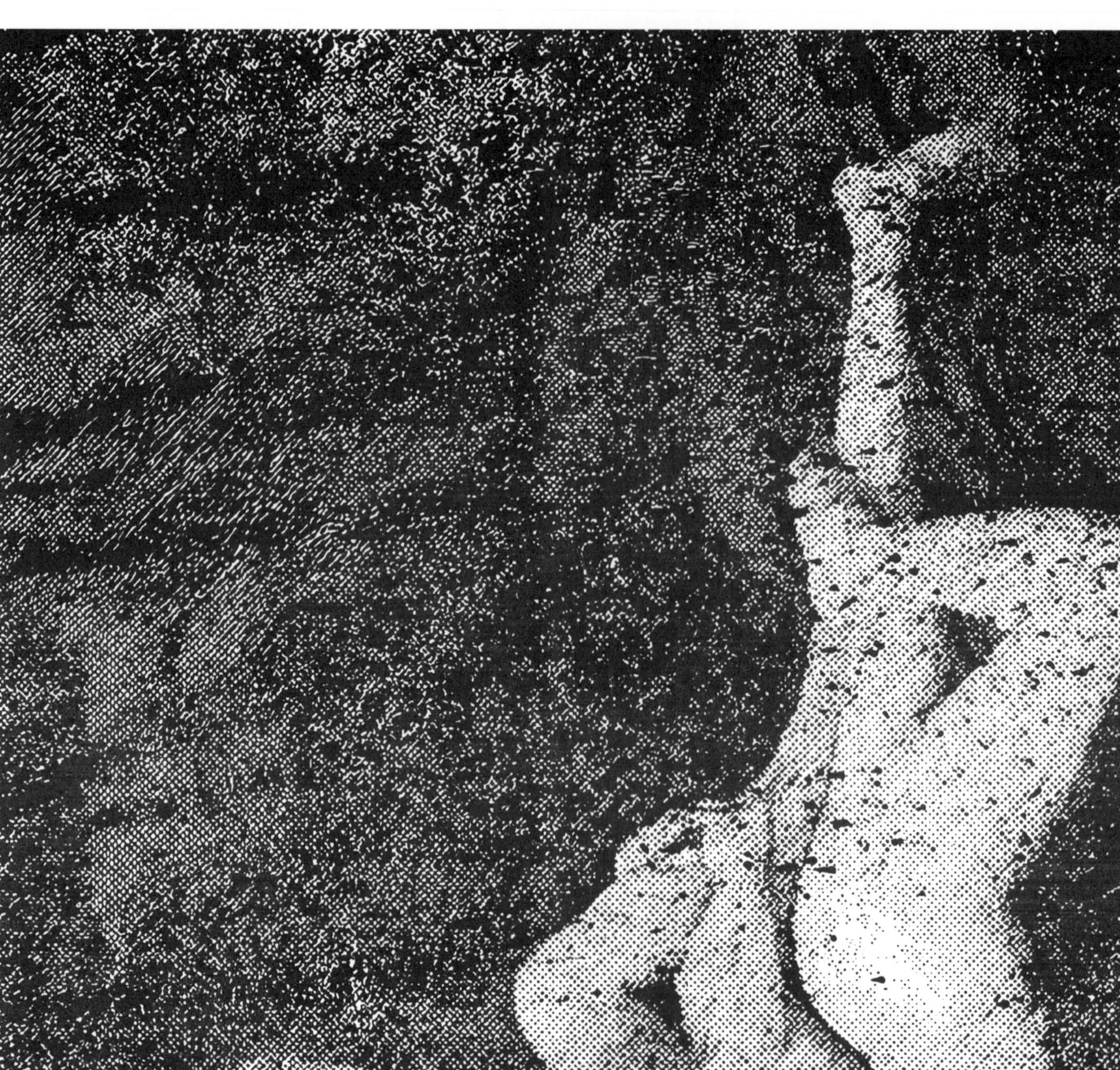

17

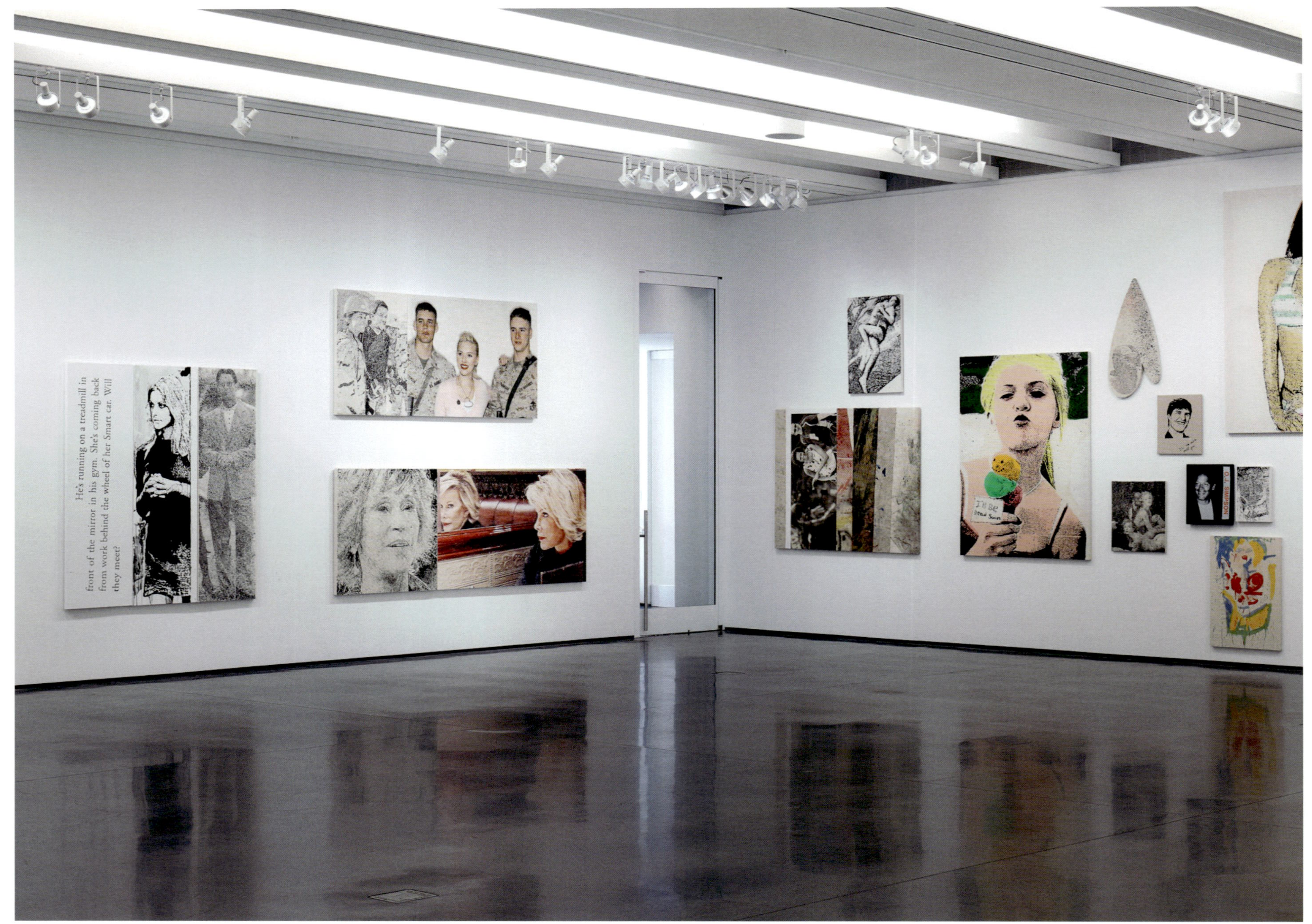

He's running on a treadmill in front of the mirror in his gym. She's coming back from work behind the wheel of her Smart car. Will they meet?

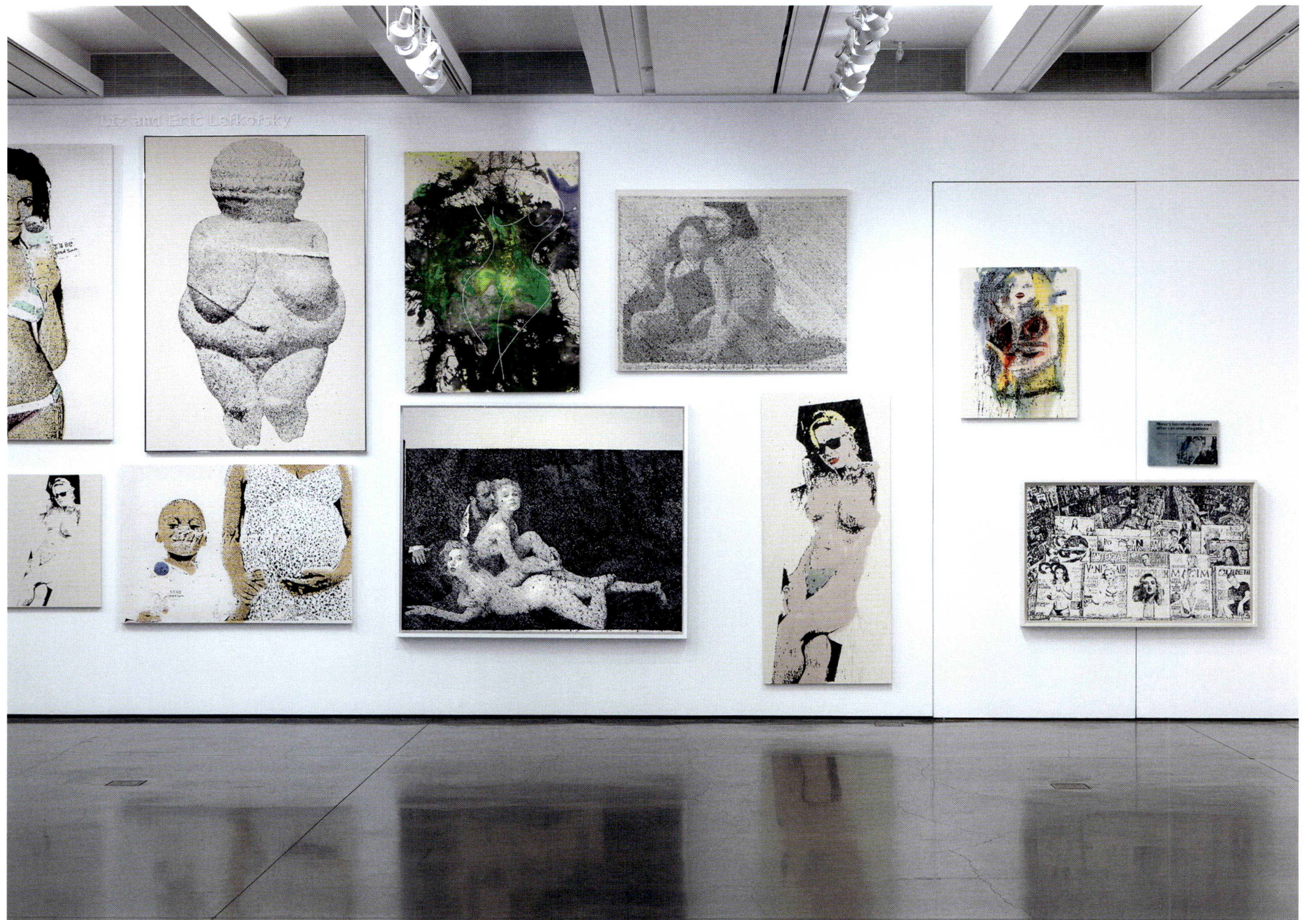
Liz and Eric Lefkofsky

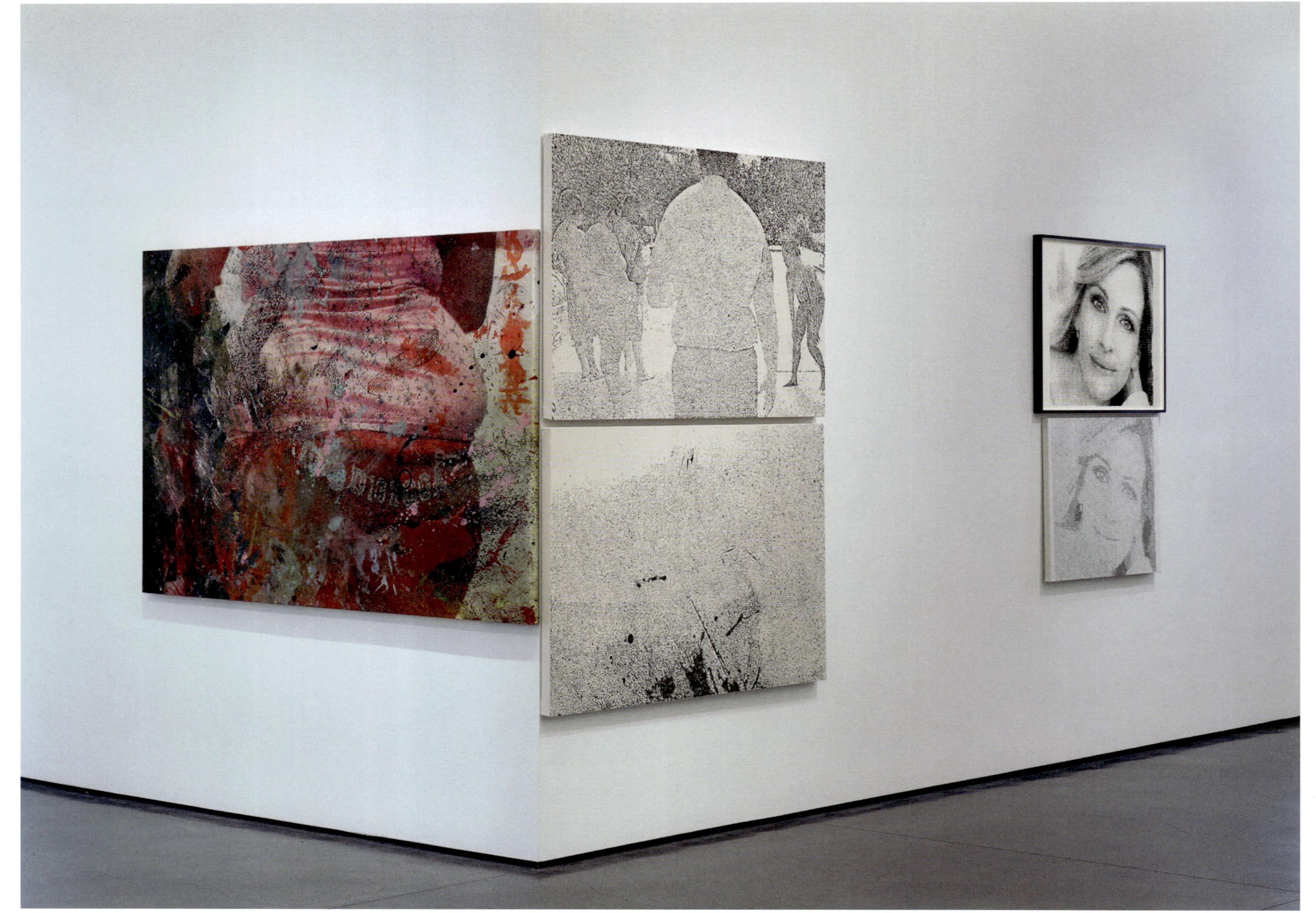

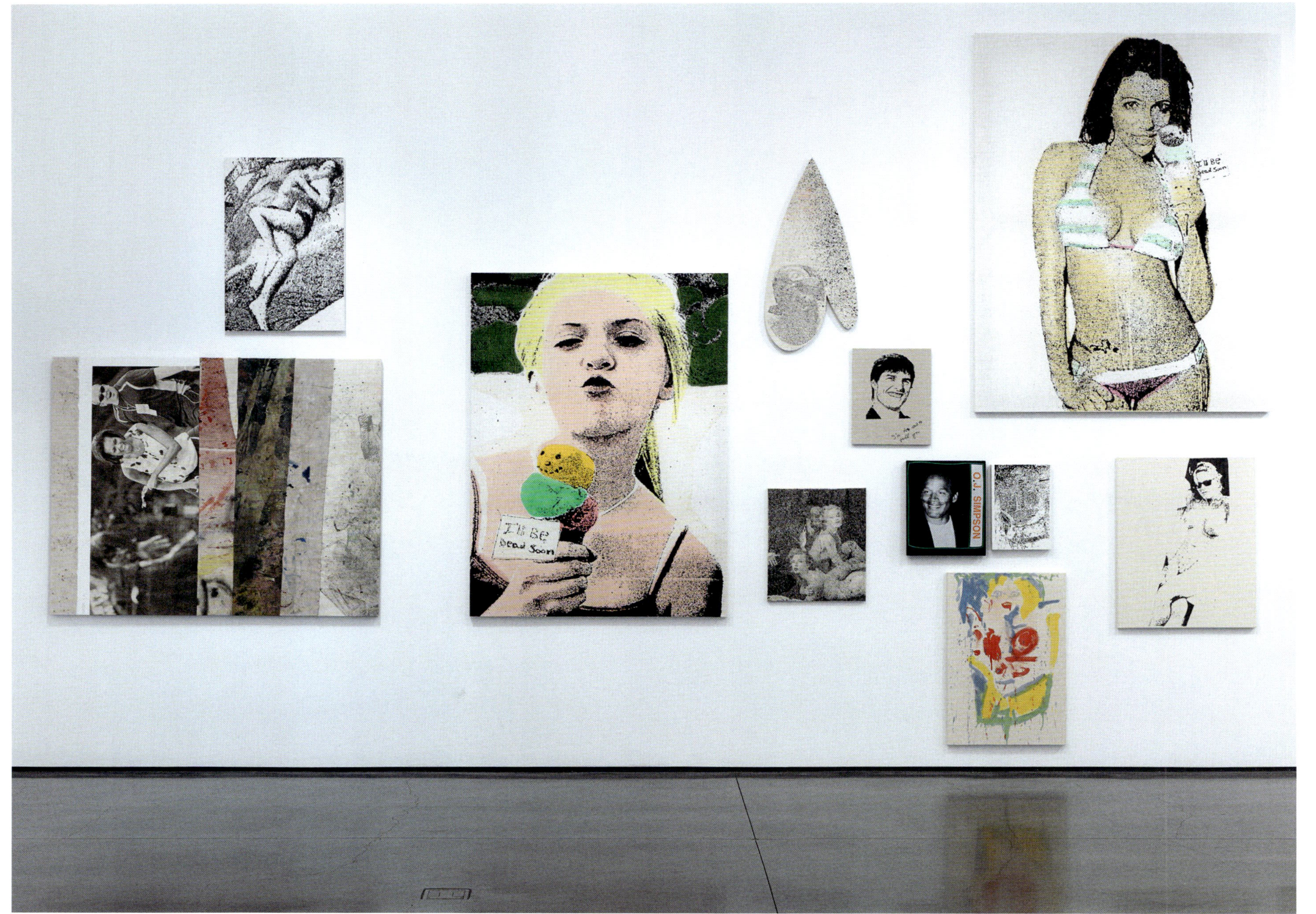

I'll Be
Dead Soon
O.J. SIMPSON
I'll Be
Dead Soon

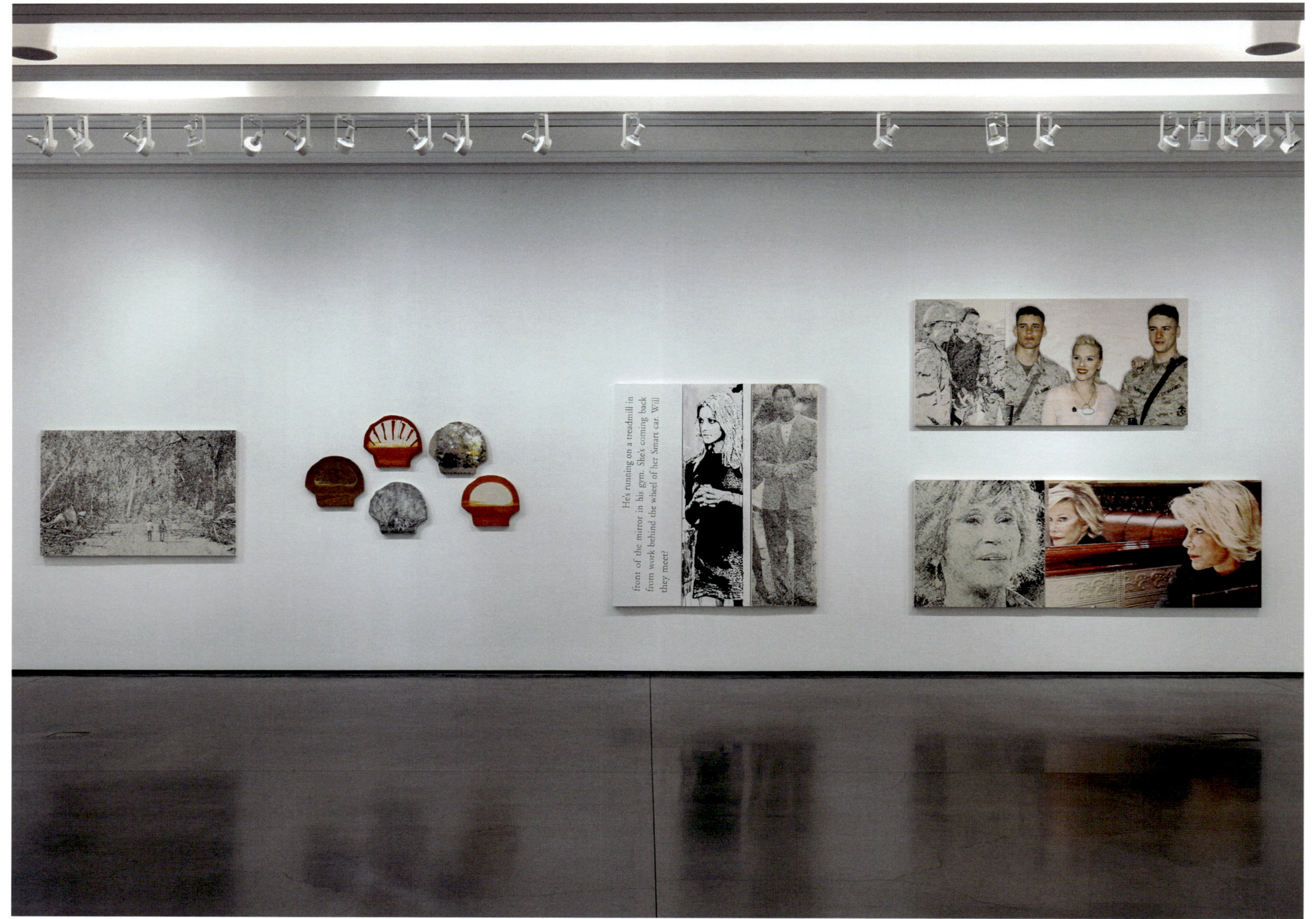
He's running on a treadmill in front of the mirror in his gym. She's coming back from work behind the wheel of her Smart car. Will they meet?

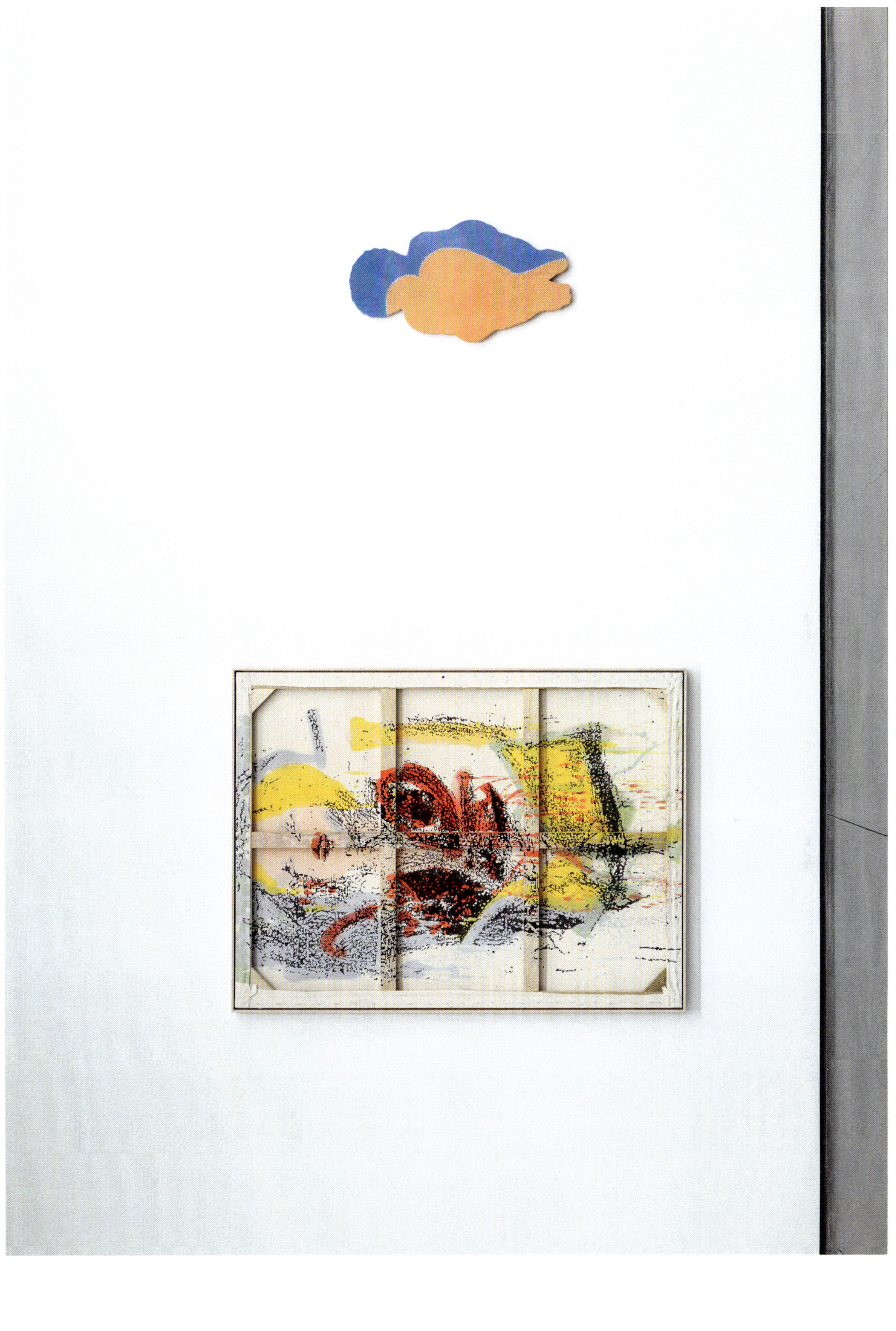

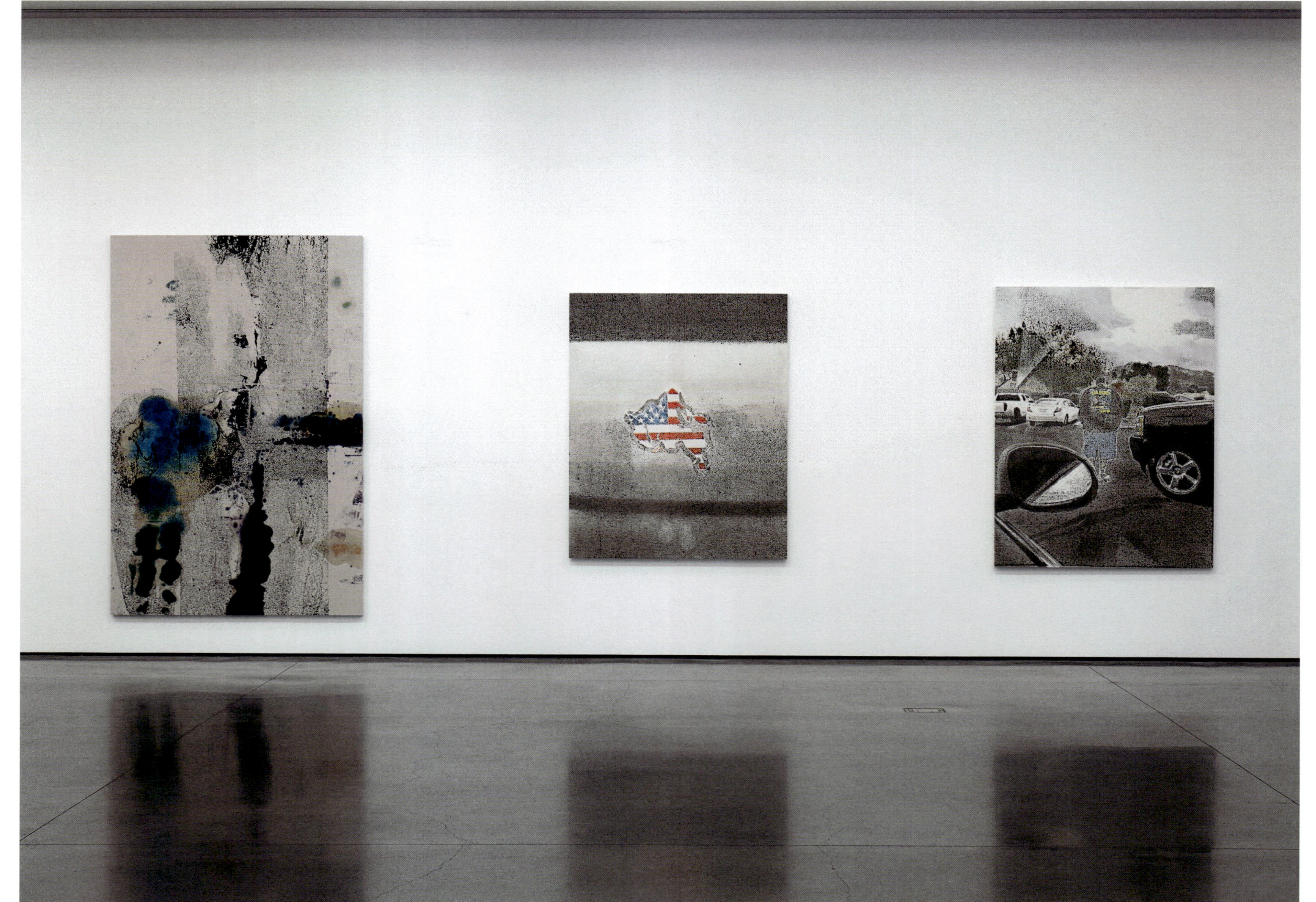

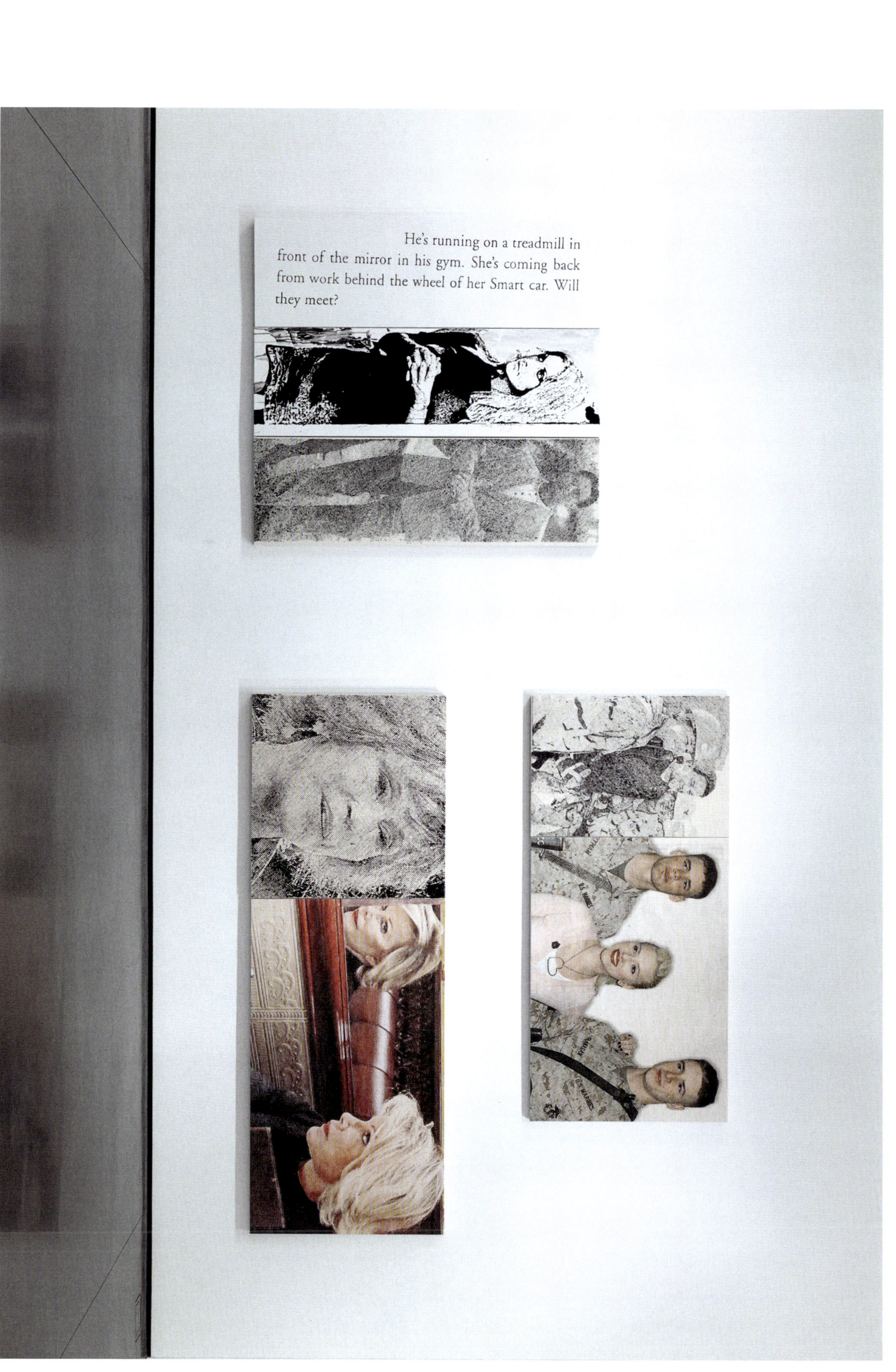

He's running on a treadmill in front of the mirror in his gym. She's coming back from work behind the wheel of her Smart car. Will they meet?

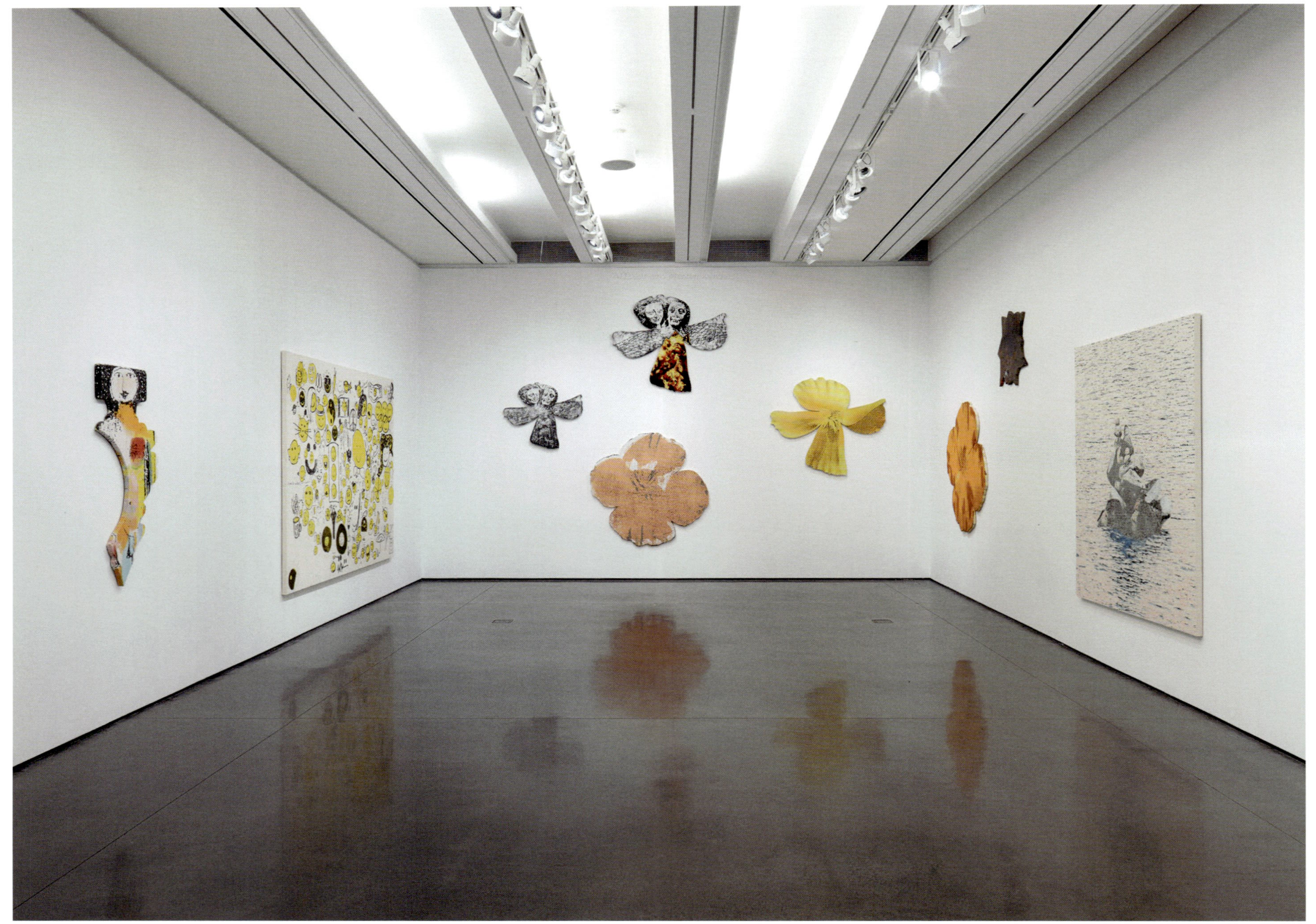

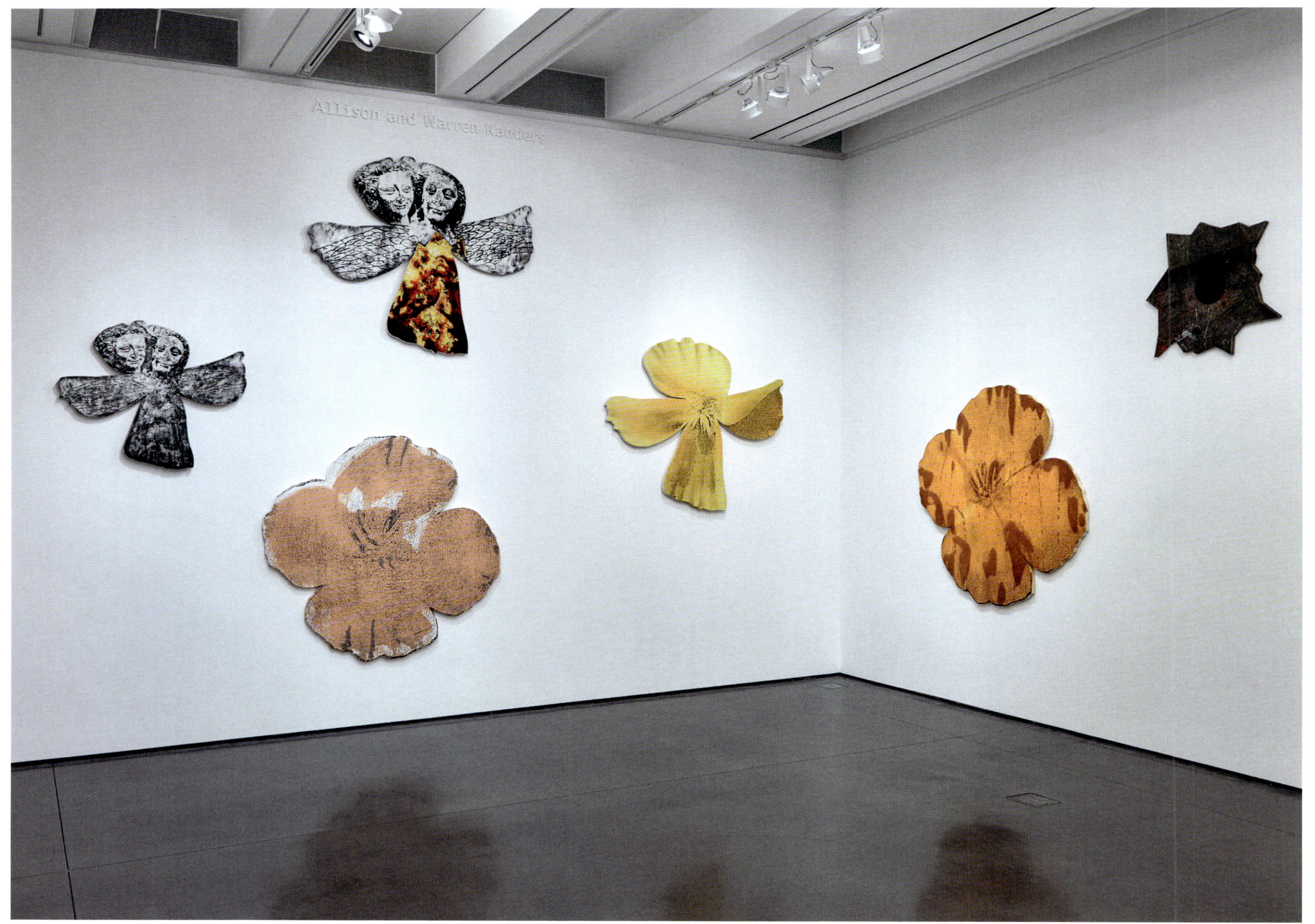
Allison and Warren Kanders

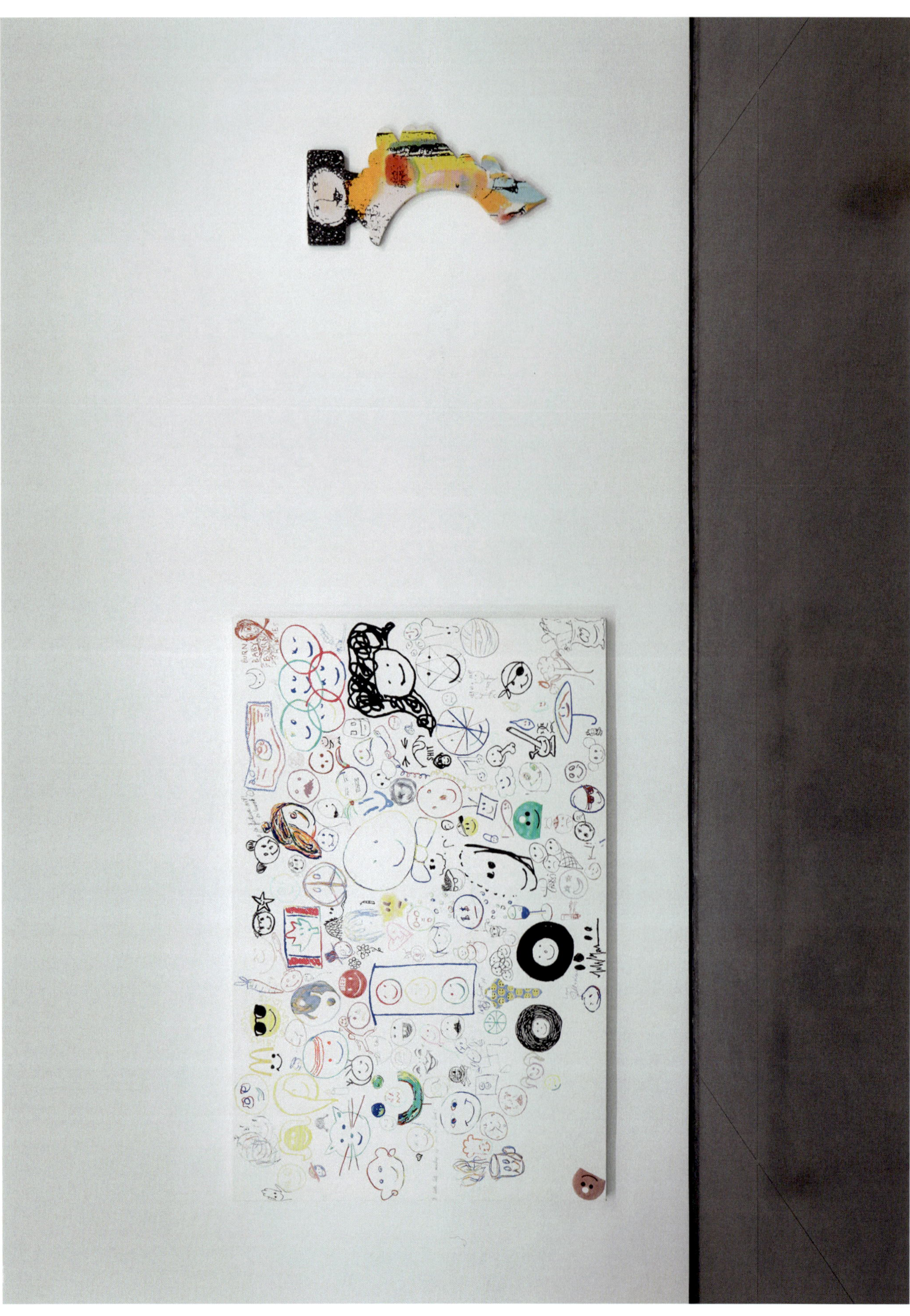

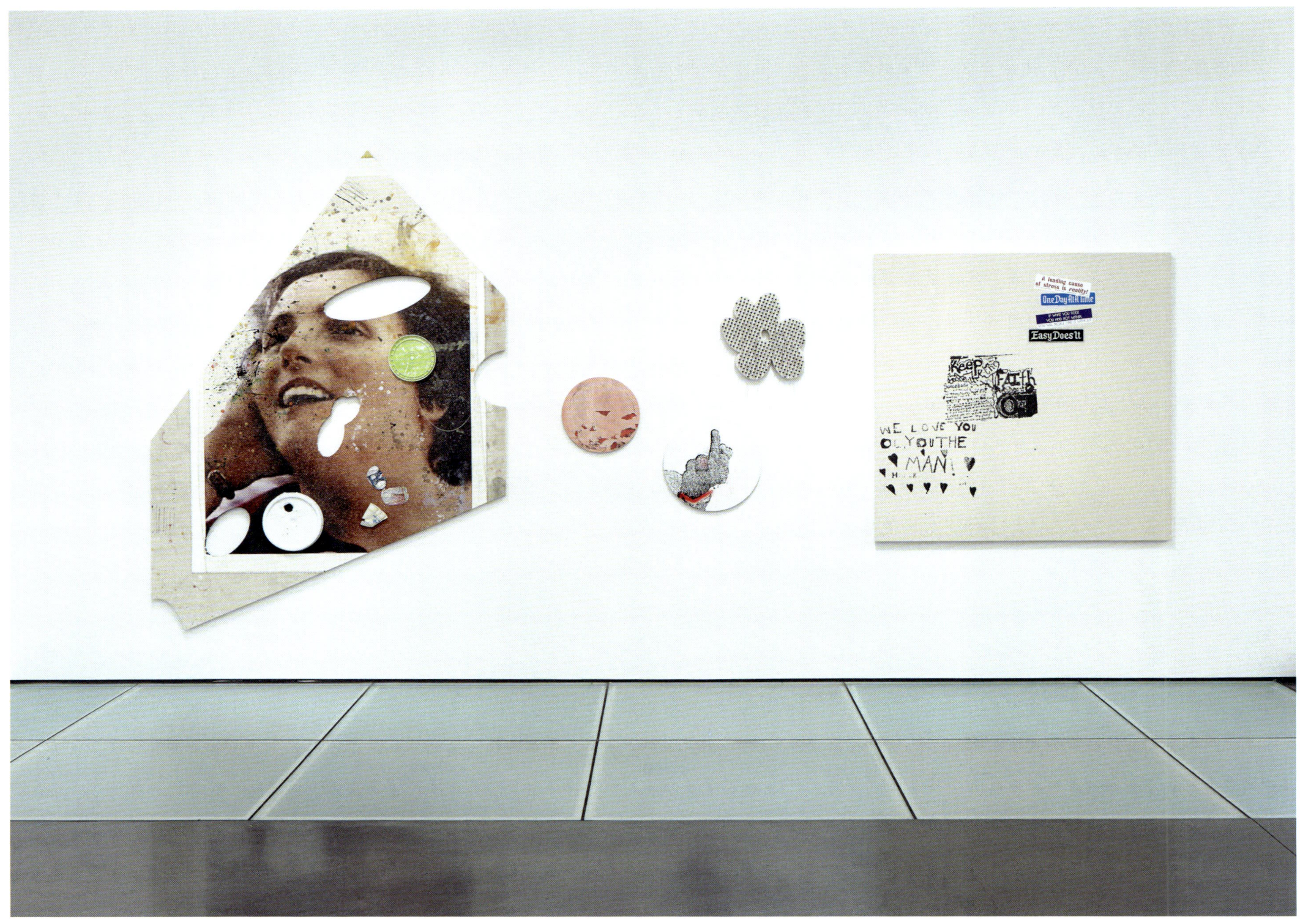

A leading cause of stress is reality!
One Day At A Time
IF WHAT YOU SEEK YOU FIND NOT WITHIN
Easy Does It
Keep FAITH
WE LOVE YOU
OL YOU THE
MAN!

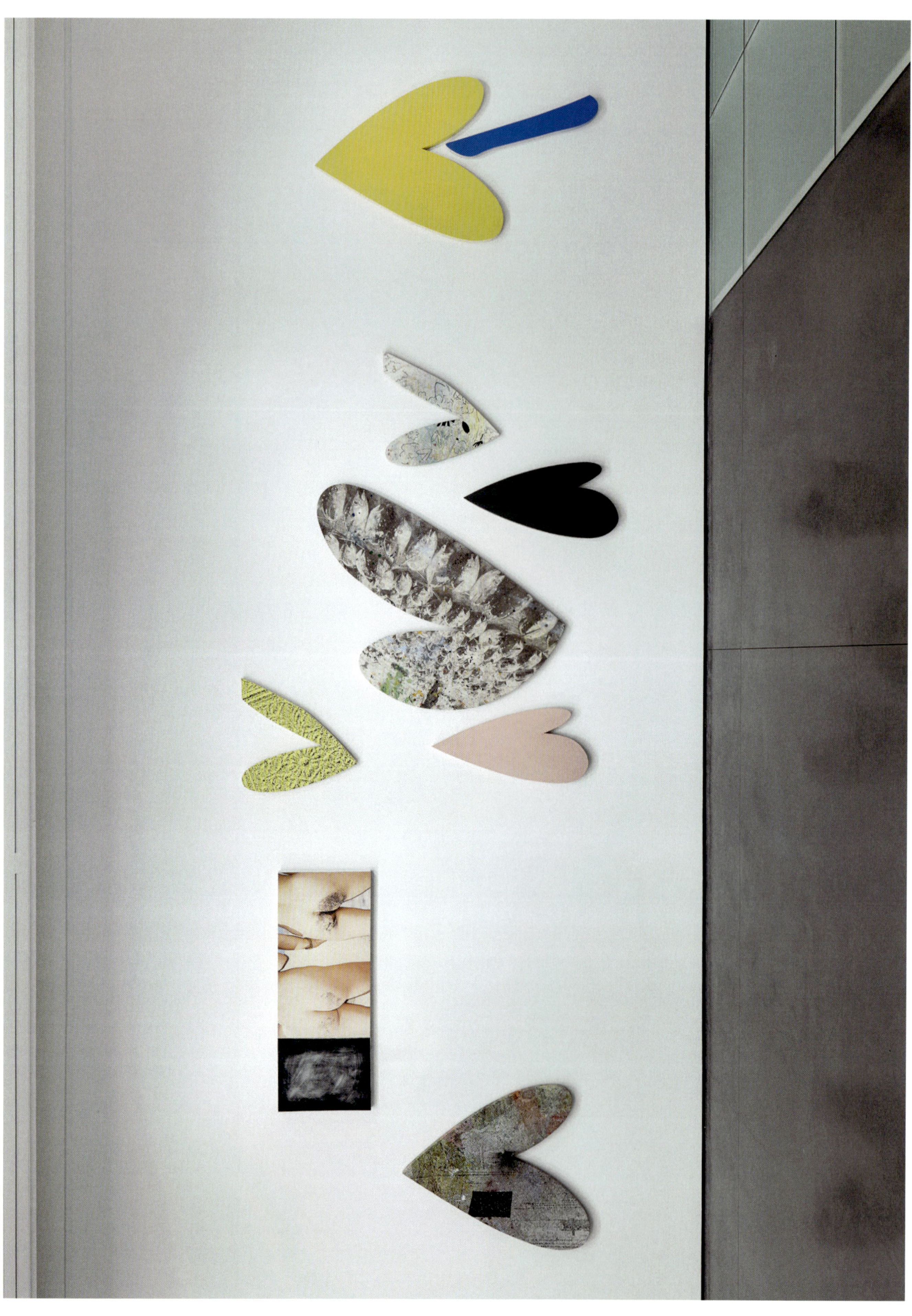

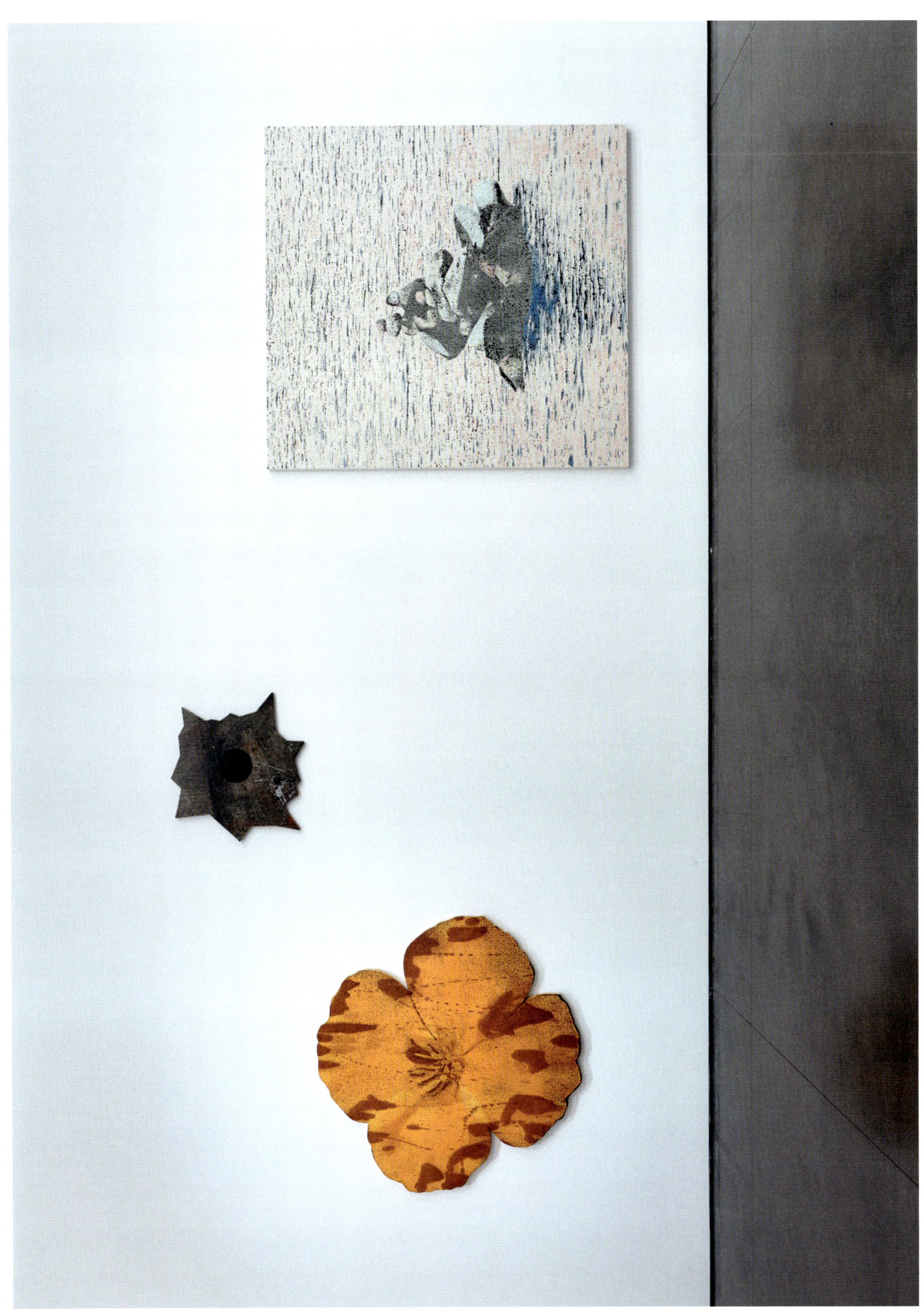

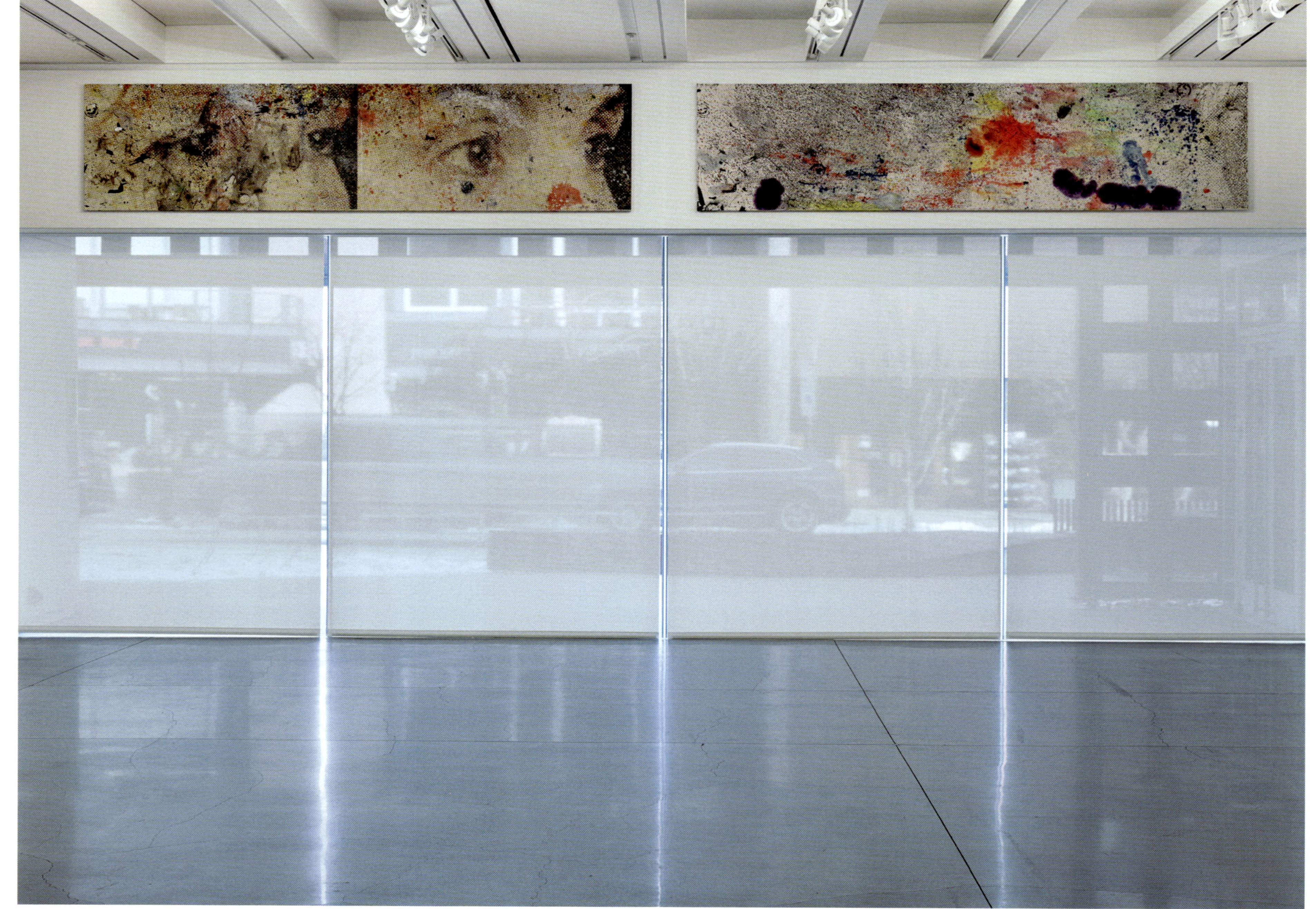

Nate Lowman: The show opened in December, right? That's five-and-a-half months ago that we left Aspen, and now the baby has teeth, and the show's still there. It's amazing.

Heidi Zuckerman: You've had this significant life change, becoming a father, and you just mentioned a very tangible way that kids help as markers of time—the way they look, their hair, teeth, size, and ability. What are the different ways it's affected you and your work?

NL   Time seems to be the most significant thing because the way I value it has changed. Also, the passing of time changes, like the way you shift gears. I experience time more quickly or slowly because my experience is shared and reflected with another person. It's not the same tempo all the time, and it's not the same as it was before. As an artist, I get to choose my own approach, which sometimes feels as though I'm working all the time and other times feels like I have no structure at all. Now, more than anything, it's about the changes—a shift of awareness of time passing. It changes everything in obvious, pragmatic ways, but I don't know if it really changes anything in my practice.

HZ   It's this amazing secret you find out once you have a kid. On some levels, it changes everything, but on other levels, it changes nothing because it's somehow natural human history. This is just what you're supposed to do.

NL   Yeah. There's a certain clarity to things I would otherwise question. That clarity simplifies some of the questions that I struggled with before. The biggest one is worrying about whether I'm pursuing happiness in proper or reasonable ways. I can dismiss that whole question now because I don't even care. I see the smile on my kid's face, and that makes me happy. I don't have to worry about whether I'm happy because it doesn't matter. That's the most liberating thing.

We get twisted up into thinking about all these stupid things over the course of our young lives because we believe we should be tending to our happiness in a way that is constructive. Maybe some people do that well, but that struggle evaporates right away when you have a kid because your priorities shift. You don't care about anything except for the happiness and well-being of this little baby—it's out of your control to a certain extent, too, but you can do your best. And you can leave yourself behind—there's a lot of freedom in that.

HZ   I've been thinking about freedom a lot and what it means to be free. Do you think about freedom within the work you produce and within the idea of being an artist?

NL   Sometimes I do, yeah. I only have a handle on it in a way that is good for making jokes that don't really mean anything. It's hard to describe. Artistic freedom often has a series of limitations imposed on it. You set yourself up so that the constraints of the media you're working with actually enable you to be free, but you are also engaged with their limitations. It's both. You're engaging in a historical language that everyone understands, and by doing that, you've imposed a structure on yourself. This could be perceived as the opposite of freedom, but it may enable you to articulate freely whatever you're trying to do.

In a philosophical sense, I'm still at a point where anytime I discover feelings of freedom, they are part of some oscillation where every epiphany feels like the breath of freedom. The mini-moments of inspiration, when I'm breaking out of something and seeing things differently, are where I experience freedom. The rest of the time, I don't think I'm particularly free. I'm stuck checking my email, held hostage by the cultural life of late capitalism.

HZ   Is there a default question that you get asked about your work all the time?

NL   One thing that people ask when they are in my studio—which is a relatively small percentage of my interactions with people—is about the way things are made. They aren't sure if my paintings are silk-screened or if they're rendered by hand. They don't believe me at first when I say I paint them by hand.

HZ   That makes sense. It's a practical question, which maybe feels safer than a conceptual one.

NL   Yeah. Conceptual thinking is where we find the things we enjoy, like freedom—which is a great idea that few of us grasp in our lifetimes—and it's really the most important aspect. Thinking is also harder to talk about articulately. As an artist who works in the studio every day, I like the practical questions because I watch paint dry all day and I love it. It's important to me. All those seemingly unimportant questions like, "What kind of tape do you use?" make vast differences in the outcome of an artwork; it can be quite nuanced, but maybe boring to talk about. Nothing is more important than the idea, because I don't even need to make the artwork, but the artwork is the way I communicate the idea.

HZ   The processes by which you make paintings have evolved, and sometimes the works are stained and stitched, but could you talk about an example of a painting that has the application of paint?

NL   Well, for *"And The Angels Are Singing But Their Skirts Are On Fire" for E.S. 2* [2017; #52], which is in Gallery 3 in the AAM show, I initially wanted to make a painting of a poppy flower that I photographed blowing in the wind. *Angel Poppy* [2016; #53] ended up being the depiction of this, which is placed right next to the one that we're talking about.

Often, when I set out to make a painting, I prepare multiple canvases for the piece, and this time, I did it in two different scales because I wasn't sure exactly which scale would be more powerful optically. I like to work on a few at the same time—if I work on three paintings, I can learn from my mistakes on the fly, and it's fun; I can go back and forth between them. It's an effective way to get one good painting if I start with two or three.

In this case, I prepared eight canvases. I was happy with the first one that came out, *Angel Poppy*. The reason I was interested in this particular flower was that if you flatten the shape, the contours resemble the angel on top of the Christmas tree. I was thinking about anthropomorphic forms coming from various parts of nature at the time. It was one in a grouping of other images, like logs that resemble legs.

So, I had a bunch of extra poppy-shaped canvases lying around for quite a while. I had done an exhibition in Reims, in France, where they make champagne. There's a remarkable cathedral there that has these funny statues of smiling angels. I spent a week there and collected the postcards from the museum. Sometimes after I return home from a trip, I'll try to make a painting of something I experienced on the trip—in a diaristic way rather than creating something to be exhibited. I added the heads from a couple of the angel images in the postcards to the poppy flower, then I drew some crude wings, which I learned from looking at stone sculpture drawings, and made a little skirt.

I also created a funny surface texture consisting of multiple coats of loosely applied house paint from Benjamin Moore, which had a layer of black latex over it. When you rub away the top coat, the black sits in the tiny brush grooves and creates this weird faux stone-ish texture. Then I painted the little angel faces, and even when I painted them loosely with drippy paint, they still retained their photographic/sculptural qualities that mimic the black-and-white postcards. It's quite fun to do, and it dries quickly because it's not oil paint, so I can do a lot in a few days. I can dry it with a hairdryer even faster if I'm bored.

So, I had this funny diaristic angel painting that was my personal, handmade souvenir of the trip. It was on my studio wall for months, and I kept looking at it. I loved it, and people would comment on it. It's not the kind of piece that I usually exhibit because it's not about anything except having been to France, which isn't very interesting relative to all the things you could be trying to communicate in the modern era. After a while, I remembered that a friend of mine, Erik, who passed away when we were young, had written this poem. There was a line in it that read, "And the angels are singing but their skirts are on fire." I realized I could combine the angels with the fire skirt, so I looked up different sources of fire. The paintings ended up becoming a memorial to Erik.

I was always fascinated by the Icelandic volcano erupting and stopping transatlantic air traffic for a period eight years ago. I loved this weird, courageous volcano that was a severe inconvenience, but super beautiful in the pictures—an orange flaming thing with chunks of lava against the northern blue light. That's one source image I used for the bottom of one of the skirts. I used oil paint, mixed the color, then thinned out the paint, so it was very diluted, stained it different colors for the fire, and then painted the charred parts over it. For another one, I used the explosion of an offshore drilling rig that had been photographed from the shore. It's this giant orange flame that turns instantly into dark smoke, but it's caught in the air. You have the smoke and the fire billowing simultaneously. That's the source image for the one that's in Aspen. It was rendered in oil paint, so it's a little more painterly than the stain.

> **HZ** You mentioned that angel painting was a memento of your trip, but wasn't enough because your paintings are always about something. Can you talk about that more?

NL Well, I'd like to think so. Maybe it's not about not being enough, but I work on lots of things at the same time, so I stumble upon interesting stuff that comes out of my daily practice in the studio. That's never not enough; it's always interesting, and I want to share it. The original endeavor of that work was a little more personal, or maybe a little more selfish or self-oriented—I wasn't setting out to communicate something specific. It seems more of a personal artifact than an artwork, but at the same time, you liked it and put it in the show. It's about my artistic intentions in that way, rather than the thing itself.

> **HZ** In general, all of your paintings have a story to tell. So, you're just explicating your intention of what went into the painting and what it does.

NL Yeah. I paint a lot from photographs that I find interesting, for various reasons. Sometimes I'll clip an image and then return to it years later—that's generally the case, in fact. I don't usually paint things right away. If I'm painting something that becomes a historical event, I typically do it with a little distance because I can approach it better. I'm not a news reporter; my painting isn't journalism. My interest comes later, not during the initial interpretation and digestion of an event.

When I paint an image from a photo, whatever it is—whether it's obscure or recognizable—the translation of going from photograph to painting is just as important as why I'm interested in the image. What's the photo about? What's the context? How has it changed? In that translation, lots of things happen: the rendering, the exchange of color, light, and all these things in the media. When it lands in the realm of painting, it can't ever leave that. It takes it somewhere else, which isn't always the best thing, but it's often interesting.

> **HZ** A key part of your practice is research, and I'm assuming you have an archiving system. How do you find the things that you set aside? How do you re-access them?

NL I have an oversized filing cabinet, which has folders in it that were originally for doctors to keep their X-rays in.

> **HZ** How are they sorted?

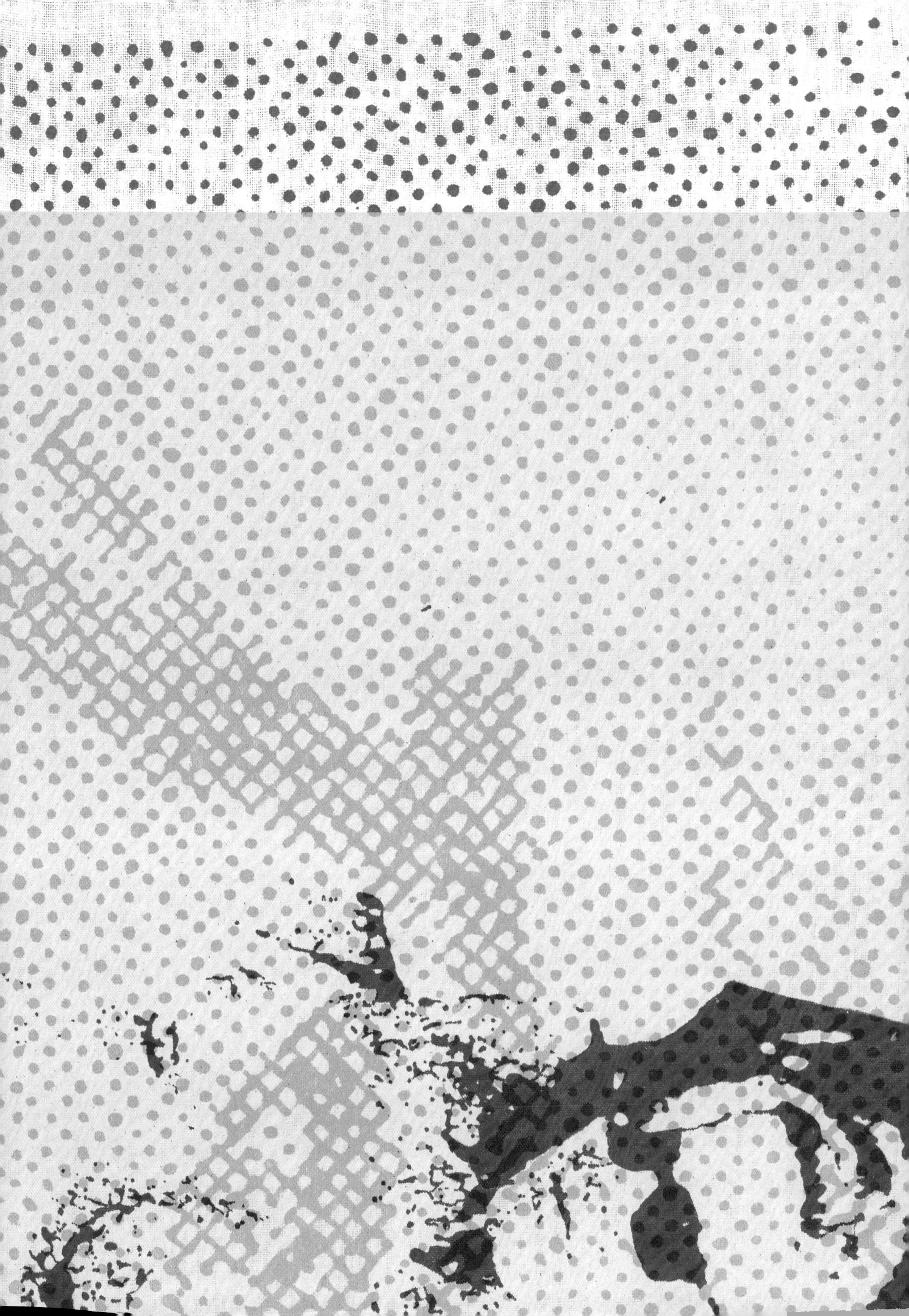

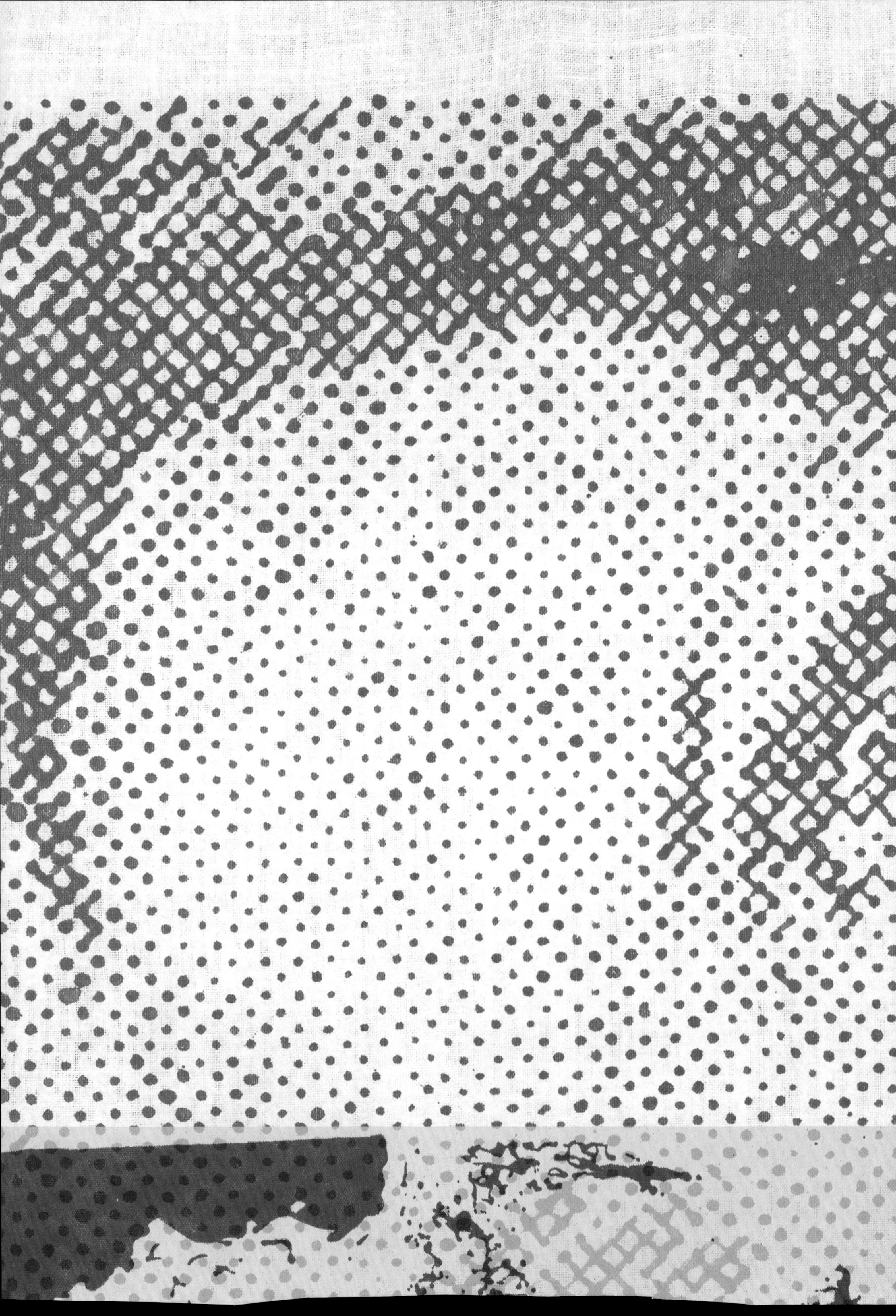

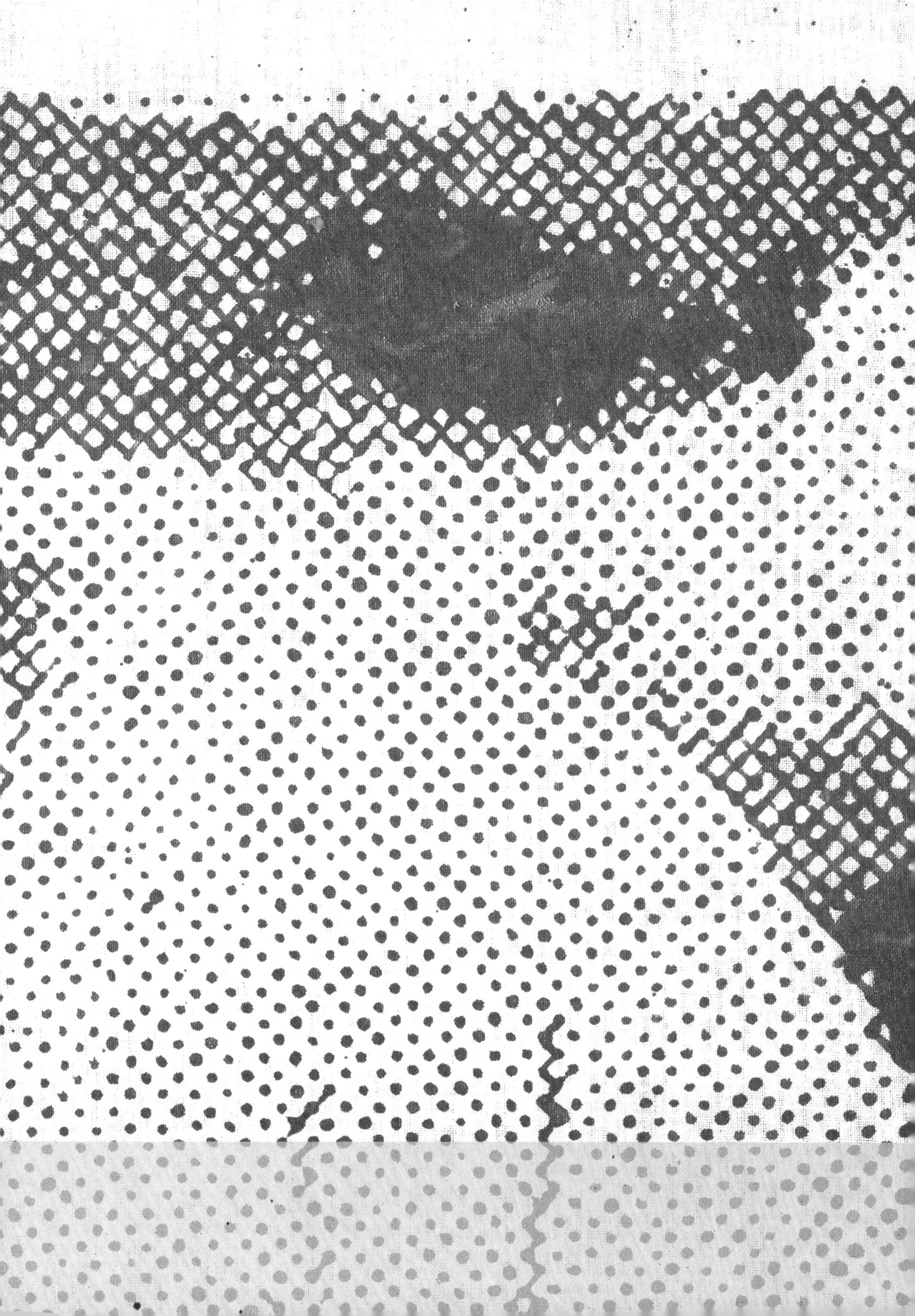

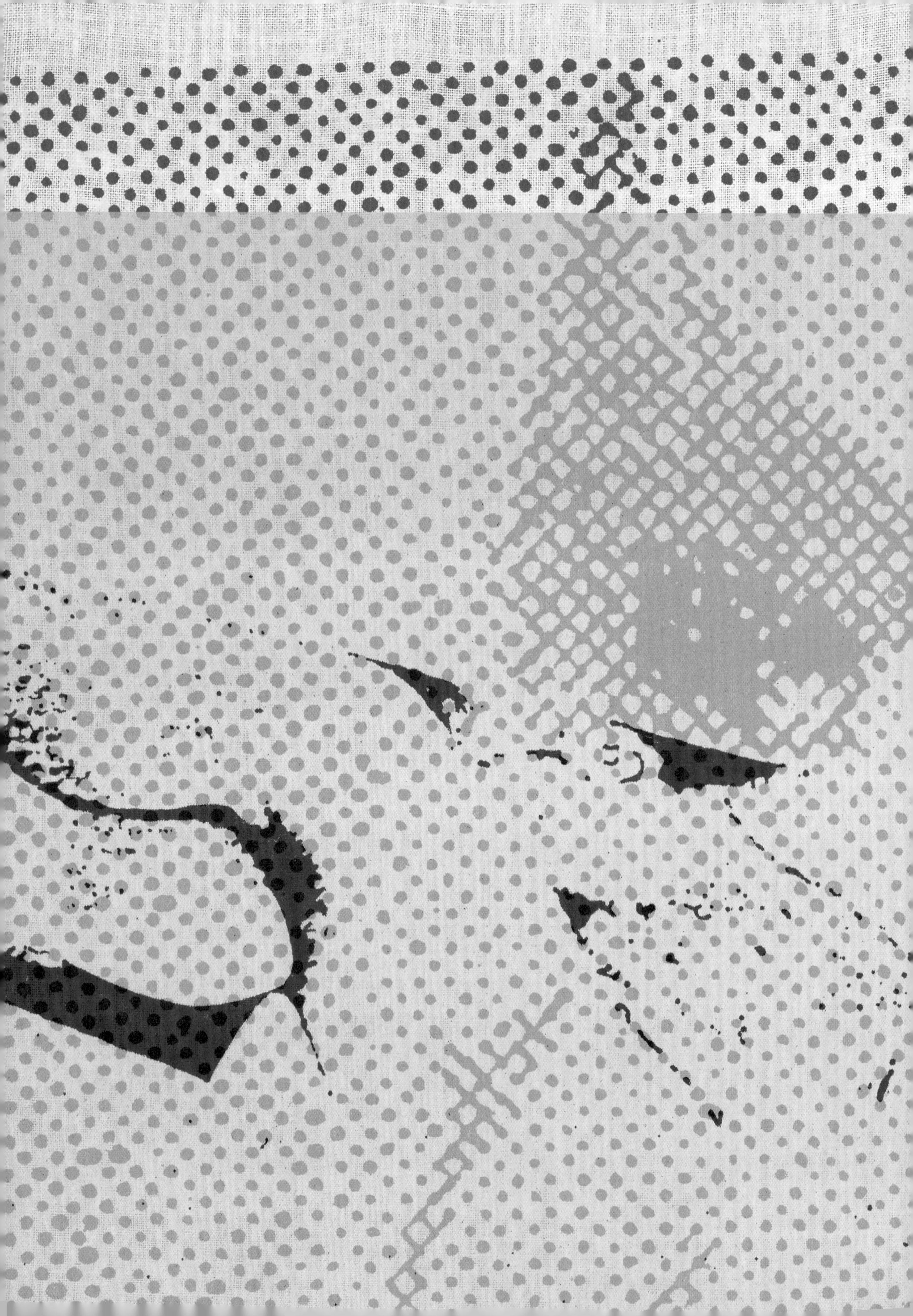

NL   Sometimes they're sorted by groupings—I'll have a loose grouping of images that I was interested in, in 2006. Anything that pertains to that over time, I clip and put in there. There was a *Before and After* file, for example.

HZ   Is it chronological?

NL   No, it's not chronological. 2006 could just be the year when I started becoming interested in something, for example, masks, clowns, makeup, or things pertaining to those. It could be anything from an image of someone wearing war paint to a Y2K funny-glasses picture. It's loose. In a way, it's quite chaotic because, four years later, I might enjoy the same image, but I'd put it in a totally different organizational file. I've had that filing unit for ten years—I have to go into it and redo it because a lot of the image groupings aren't ones I particularly care about anymore.

One of the files was called "Parades and Funerals." It was about processions and get-togethers with flowers, umbrellas, and crowds. Printed photographs of funerals are usually for someone well known, so images of private funerals don't normally end up in a magazine or newspaper. I don't think I've added anything to that file in six years—I haven't even looked at it. There were also some interesting images of Olympic ceremonial performers from Korea, which might be interesting to look at now, but maybe only a glance. To say that it's organized only pertains to me—if I asked someone to find a picture, they wouldn't be able to.

HZ   It gives a lot of insight into your practice and the way that you think, organize, and filter.

NL   My research is very bingey. I go for periods of time where I don't put a lot of effort into it—which isn't to say that there isn't an automatic process of collecting information. Going down a certain research road, I end up using more specific criteria than I do when I'm just receiving information on a day-to-day basis, and I need both.

HZ   I often resist categorization—I wonder why people need to compartmentalize to understand. I like an open, expansive way of being and thinking. But I do like these little synopses. Last night, someone was talking about why works of art go to auction, and they explained it was the three Ds: debt, divorce, death. My response was that, when we're looking for people to serve the museum, we look for the three Ws: wisdom, work, and wealth. He then said, "Oh, yeah. In business, there are the three Is: innovators, implementers, and idiots." It's like playing poker: I see your three Ds, and I up you three Ws—they're just different ways of thinking about the world.

I want to ask you about repetition because you often make paintings on the same or a similar subject. You talked a little bit about how, if you make three at the same time, you can learn in real time about what you're doing. Can you talk about the *Marilyn* paintings [#39–41] in relation to this?

NL   With those paintings, I was trying to teach myself how to stain in the color. This was also the case when I painted the Toys "R" Us sign, but changed "Toys" to "Generous," and stained a bunch of coats of different colors on the canvas. The "Generous" piece is a funky painting, but I was pleased with it. It has all these oily marks from the turpentine, but I liked the way the staining looked. It's substantially confusing because I articulated the shape of the letters, but it's stained with this juicy paint—the hard edges and soft stain confuse people momentarily. It's not so slick that people don't know, but there's a moment where the entry point that people use to understand the language of the painting is masked a tiny bit—they question whether it's painted or printed. It makes it more interesting, even if it's less clear, and might keep people involved slightly longer.

From time to time (and more so when I was younger), one of the things I get confused about is my life as an artist. Given that I am in charge of constructing my life, and delivering the meaning of it to people, there is always this struggle to keep it away from being this selfish endeavor and keep it more, or all, on the generous side. Sometimes I don't know whether I live a selfish or generous life.

I made the "Generous" painting in 2009. Before that, in 2005, I made a tiny copy of Willem de Kooning's *Marilyn* in a diptych with a stretched T-shirt of OJ Simpson [#26]. That piece is in the Aspen show. I made it because I wanted to address violence toward blond women—I thought de Kooning's painting was particularly violent against his subject, Marilyn Monroe. I likened the activity of that action painting to OJ stabbing his blond ex-wife. It was a dark joke I wanted to make when I was twenty-six years old. The canvases of the diptych aren't the same size; they don't even line up.

My first rendering of the de Kooning is just black from a shitty photocopy of the original. It looks ugly, but I really enjoyed it. Making two paintings of a photocopy of somebody else's painting isn't the kind of thing you do, but I thought there was something I could investigate further someday. When I learned how to paint with the stain, I decided to try to do a two-phase rendering of the de Kooning, copy his colors, stain them where they're stained, and then add the photocopy on top. I got three canvases because I didn't know what I was doing and was cautious at first. Eventually, by the third one, I was slopping the paint on like I was a regular old 1940s Abstract-Expressionist guy.

All three of those first ones ended up being as good as one another, so I decided to have a trilogy of paintings. They were called *Anger Management Trilogy 1, 2,* and *3*. Then I had this crazy desire to make more. I hadn't set out to make a series, but when the third one finally came out well, it was just exciting. De Kooning makes some wonderful colors, and I was just copying them, but it was fun to paint with them—even if I got it wrong.

Then it became about doing this same thing over and over. What were the slight variations? How was that interesting? I developed a certain ritual around it. I would set up a handful of canvases at a time, my assistant would help me mix the paint, and then we painted them with projectors, so I would turn the lights down fairly low and turn the music up. We'd do it at night and go quite late. It was really fun, listening to our favorite music, and he'd hand me the cans of paint and tell me if I missed a spot. When you're younger, you think, "I'm going to be an artist when I grow up because I want to be doing that."

HZ   You're in the zone.

NL   Right. It's not what life's like as an artist, but for those hours at a time, it was fucking partying. It was crazy. I would do them in little batches from time to time until I felt exhausted. I used to half-joke that this is the closest I'll come to being a serial killer, because you do it over and over the same way.

HZ   Yeah, process and repetition.

NL   Yeah.

HZ   In your show in Aspen, when there are figures in your work, they're almost all women. How would you respond to that?

NL   Yeah. That must be your fault. No, I'm just kidding. I don't know.

HZ   Do you think that's true of your overall practice?

NL   No, I don't think so. We could divvy it all up, and you might be right. I don't know. It's interesting. I guess maybe I'll find out and tell you. It could be true. The angels are sexless. I referred to one of the angels as a "she" once, and a French visitor got after me about the angel being a man.

HZ   Really?

NL   Yeah. In my own studio.

HZ   You've also worked with cars, air fresheners, and bumper stickers. Are you interested in car culture? Do you think it's an inherently American thing?

NL   Well, the car culture I'm interested in is similar to most things. It's taken to a certain extreme in America and has its own performative identity. I'm not interested in traffic or specialized car culture…I'm interested in why cars are more and more ugly every year. It's insane. Everybody goes along with it like it's OK. And they're all the same—Bentleys all look slightly rounder and more aerodynamic in a fake way that doesn't make sense. You have to get an old car.

Anyway, my interest in car culture is actually more because I grew up in southern California. You spend so much time on the road in between places. If you live in Los Angeles, you have to go for a drive just to take a walk. It's bullshit. I grew up in a town that was around a mountain, so we didn't have to go anywhere to take a walk. But everywhere else, there are cars sitting on massive freeways with one person per car, usually, and all the windows rolled up. There might be five thousand people in a very small vicinity, but they're all alone and would never talk to each other. Maybe they have a bumper sticker about their cat or Jesus, and that's their way of communicating. I've always liked the found language, the stupid fonts, and the colors of those stickers. I thought of them as similar to Jenny Holzer's *Truisms*, but manufactured, non-poetry, true-statement versions. I was interested in how those might work in an artistic language, in painting. My bullet-hole paintings came from magnets that you put on a car to make it look as though somebody shot at it. The air freshener came later.

HZ   Is there anything you struggle with as an artist?

NL   Yes. Hmm. Is there anything *you* struggle with?

HZ   Not as an artist, of course, but yes, all sorts of things. Less and less now, honestly, but probably self-doubt is the biggest thing for me.

NL   Most of my struggles are emotional ones that are as pertinent to living in New York or America or planet Earth today as they are being an artist. Being an artist and a father are the two good parts. Having said that, making art can be difficult—well, not difficult, but it's not easy.

HZ   A lot of the people in your work have come into the cultural consciousness—not necessarily because they are celebrities, but because something happened to them. Do you have a perspective on fame and celebrity, personally as well as how it relates to your work?

NL   Yeah. I was more interested when I was younger because it was the beginning of celebrity culture. There was a shift happening in the news, in journalism, and in general perception that was driven by a cult of celebrity. Celebrities themselves, as people, as subjects, are almost lost completely—talk about lack of freedom. I was interested in the machinations of media and information, rather than in people for who they are or why they're famous. It was more about the stuff that their figure would hold, like collective insanity—which is, in a personal way, very unfair to those subjects because it doesn't have anything to do with them as people. It has to do with a collective misinterpretation of people, information, incidents.

I'm not sure if I have those interests anymore, only because the way we live with information has changed. To engage with those kinds of subjects the same way feels nostalgic or from a different time. It would be irrelevant. A lot of the images I was working with in the past were printed, for instance, which is an entirely different thing. Since around 2010, the newspaper itself, which we used to consider a two-dimensional form of information with pictures and letters, is now just a sculpture.

> HZ   I hadn't thought about that, but because there is so much social media, TV, and there are still newspapers, this whole notion of celebrity has dissipated. You can almost hide in the sheer volume of information that's out there. There isn't one news cycle anymore. It's just so pervasive and populated.

NL   It's a very fast-moving amnesia machine.

> HZ   Exactly. I've always been fascinated by the stories that would capture the headlines and then be gone entirely. Like the family that disappeared—I guess because they died. Or that girl who disappeared on her high school trip in Bermuda. And the story of the Dutch guy who killed her has come back a few times because he assaulted more people. Often, they do come back in the headlines if they're solved, but some things just completely disappear.
>
> I was just in Southeast Asia, and on one of the flights, we couldn't take off because someone had checked their bags in, but didn't get on the plane. After searching for the luggage, they found and removed six bags in total. Then the person next to me leaned over and said, "I don't want to find out where that missing Malaysia Airlines plane went." I was like, "What are you talking about? Don't say that to me." I had completely forgotten about that plane. That's another story where things just vanish.

NL   I remember it, because that plane disappeared and, at the same time, those hundreds of girls got kidnapped. Those things feel like ancient history, but it was less than five years ago. It feels as old as the Pan Am flight that was bombed over Scotland. It's totally psychotic.

> HZ   Yes, time itself is now somehow completely different to understand; amnesia, irrelevance, and meaning all factor in.

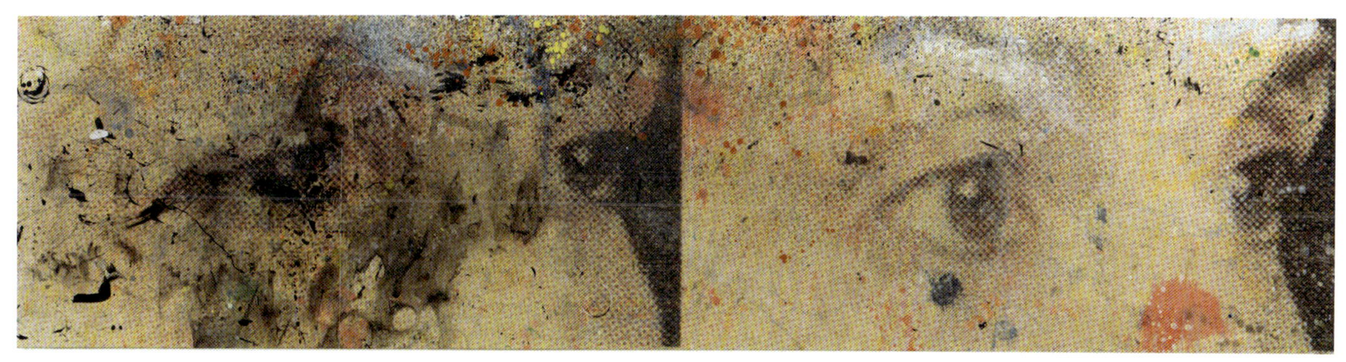

1

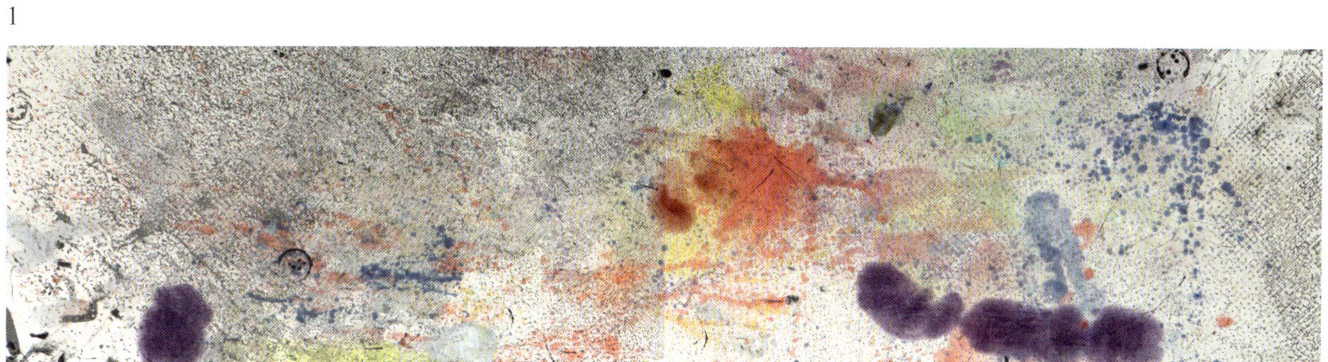

2

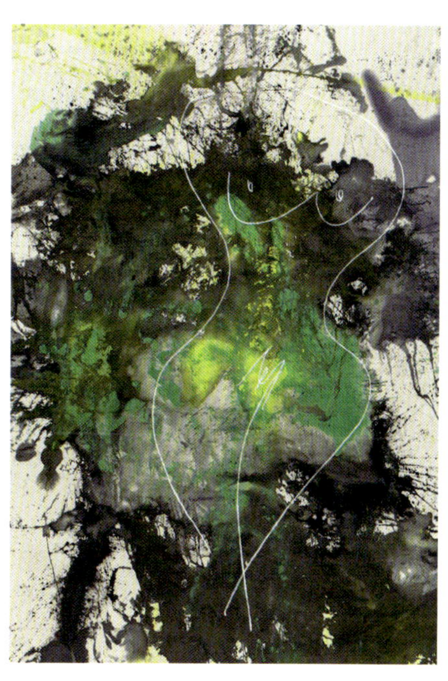

3

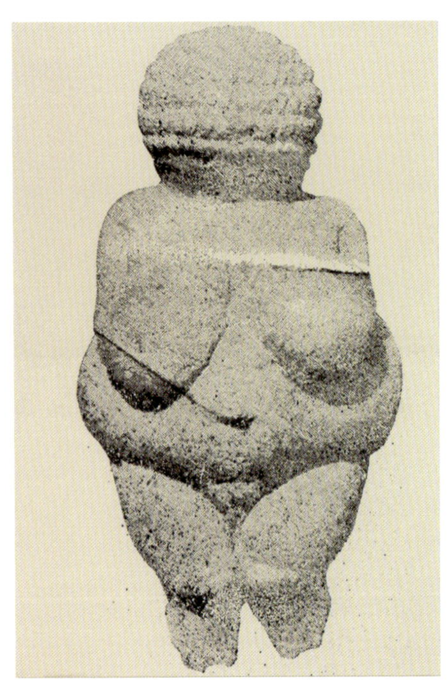

4

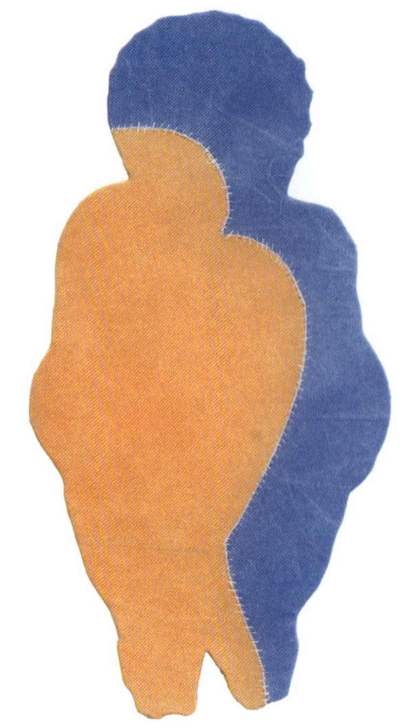

5

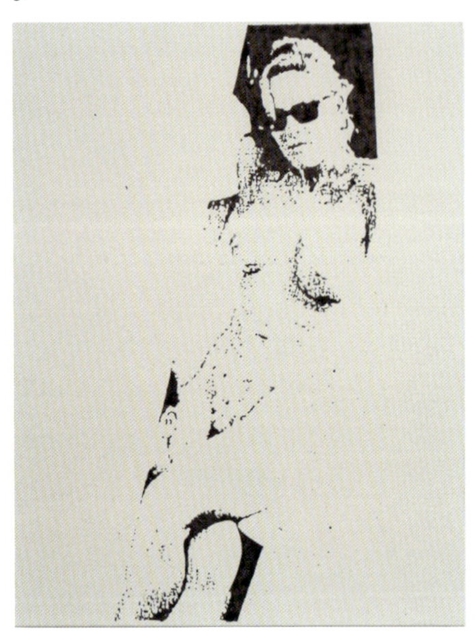

6

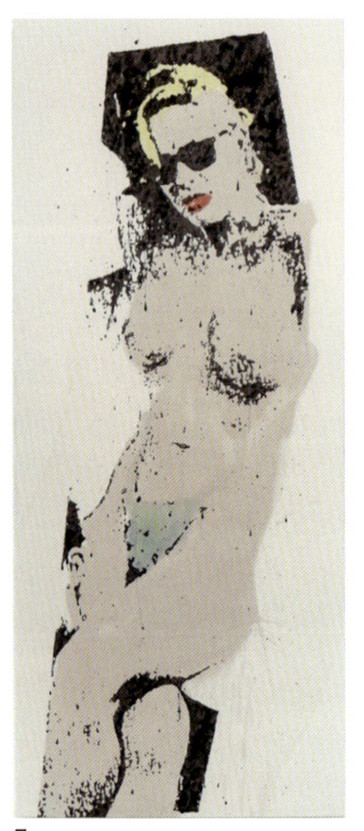

7

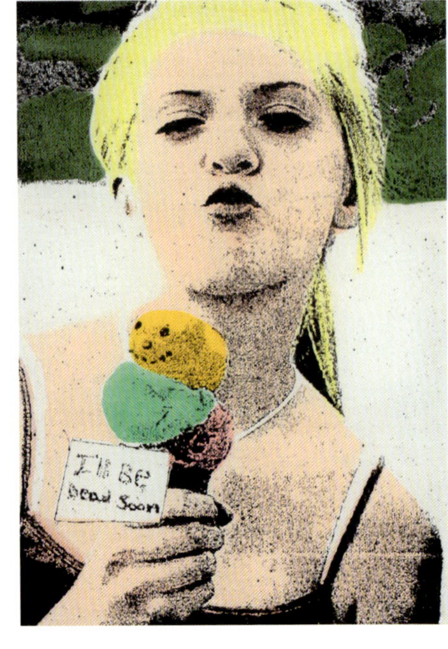

8

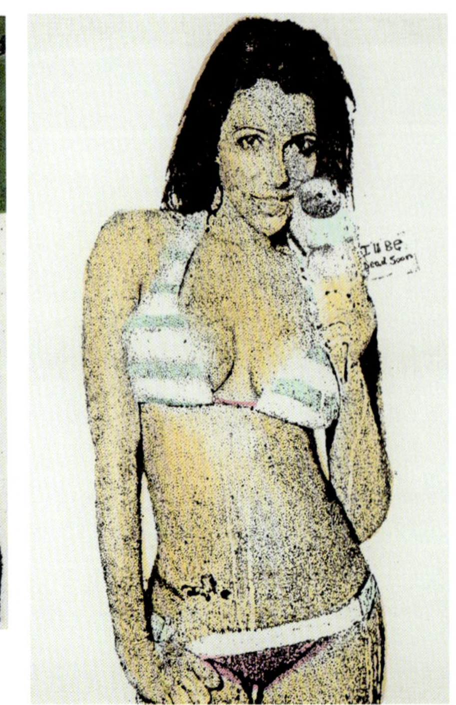

9

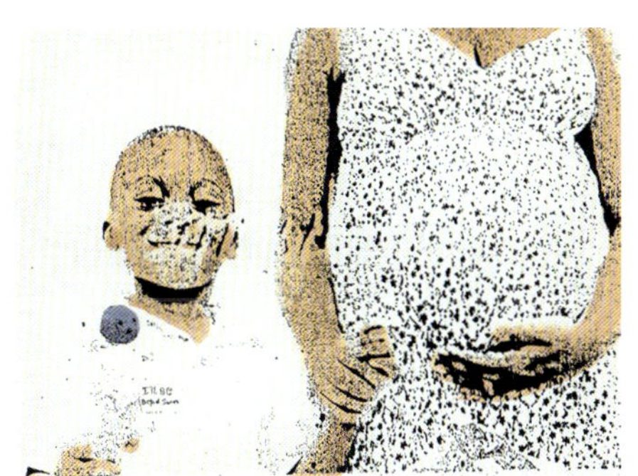

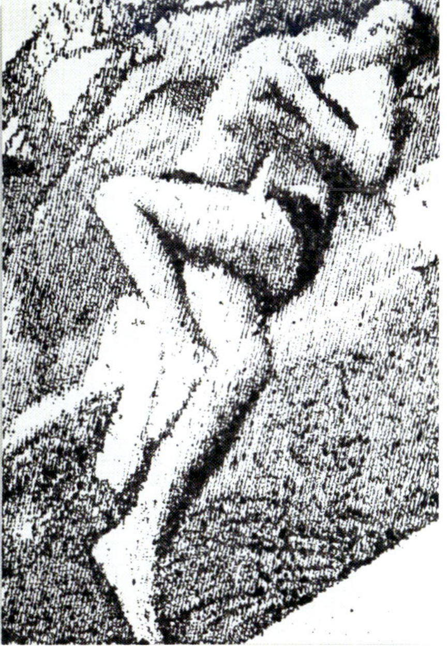

10

11

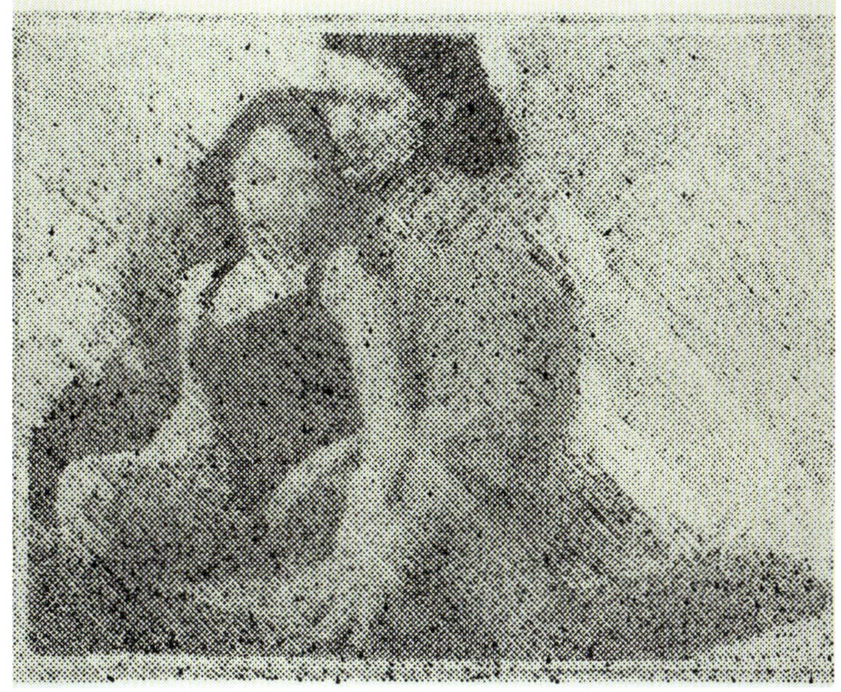

12

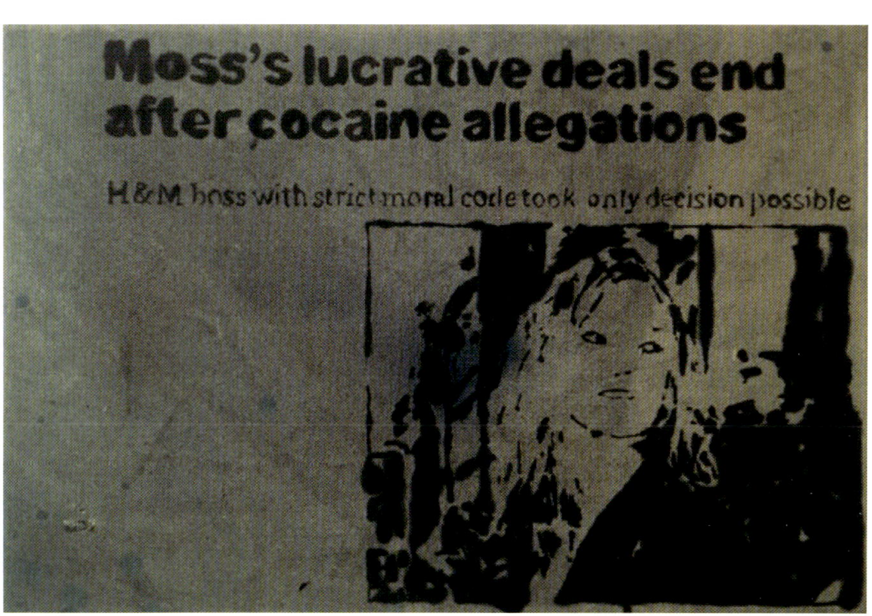
Moss's lucrative deals end after cocaine allegations
H&M boss with strict moral code took only decision possible

13

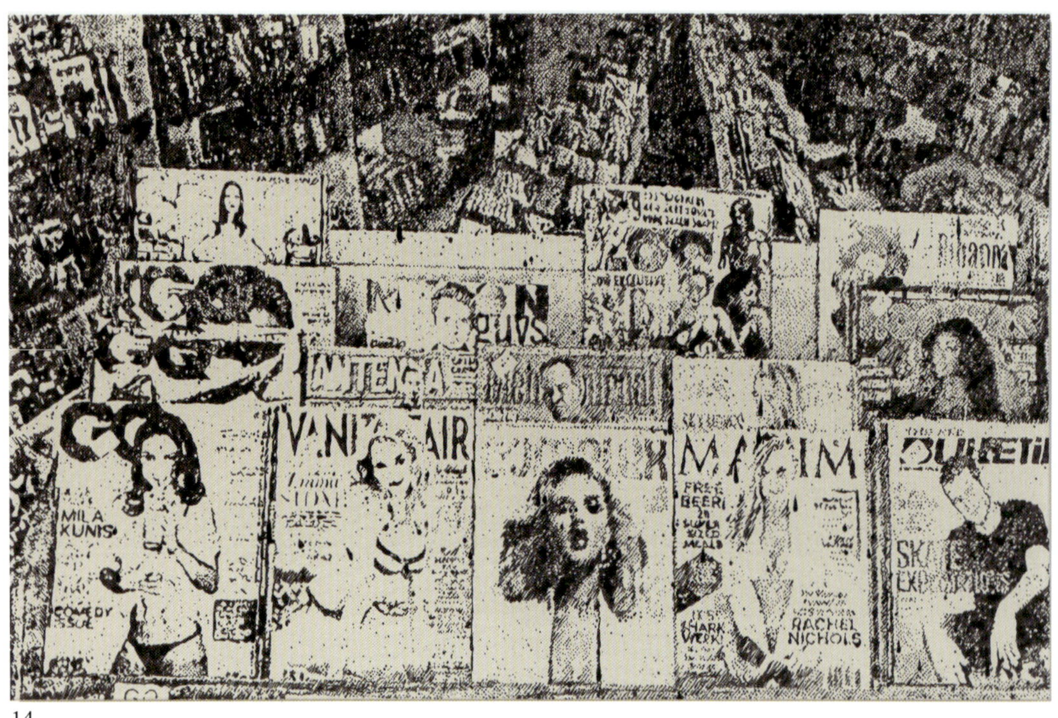

14

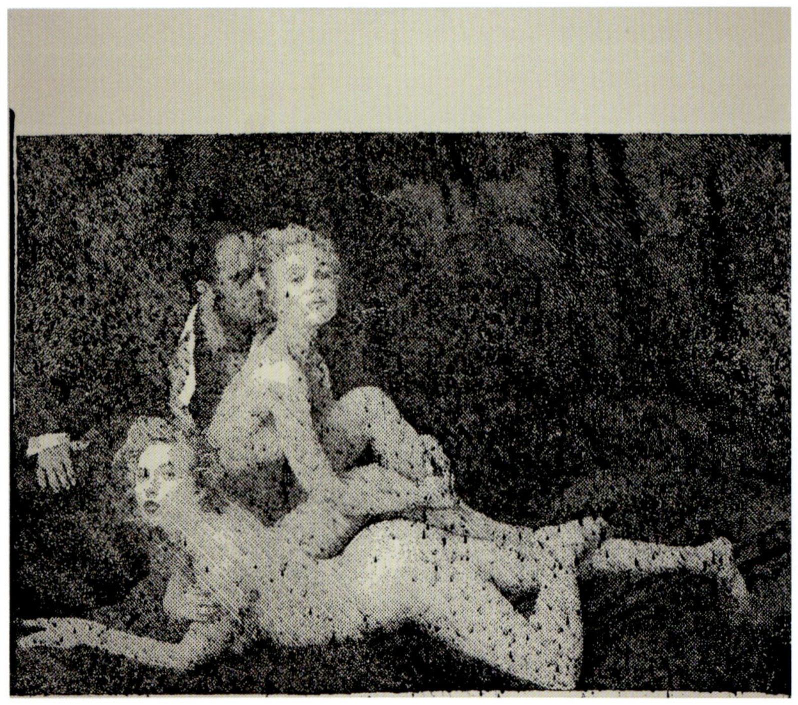

15

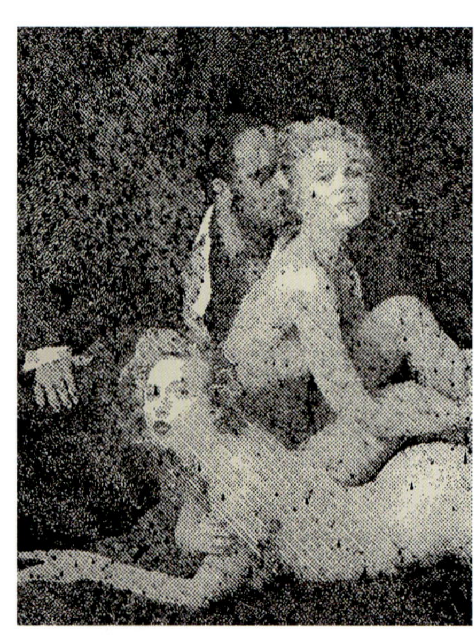

16

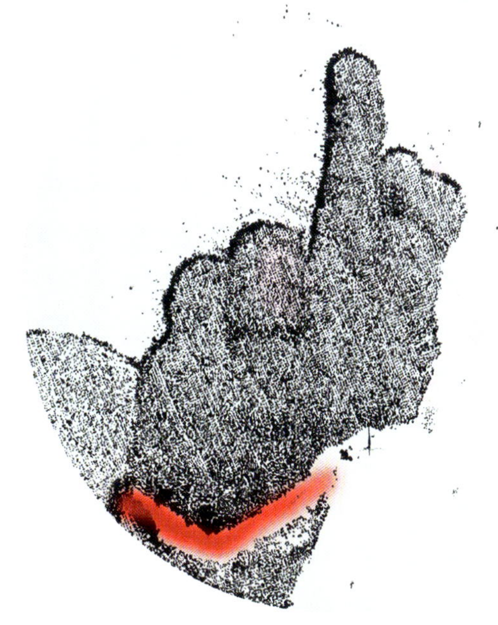

17

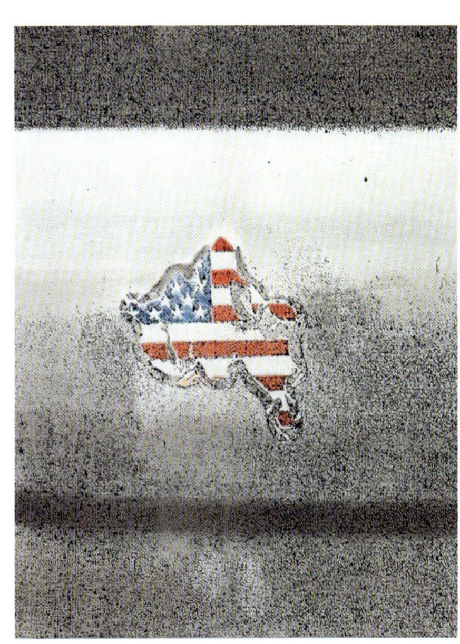

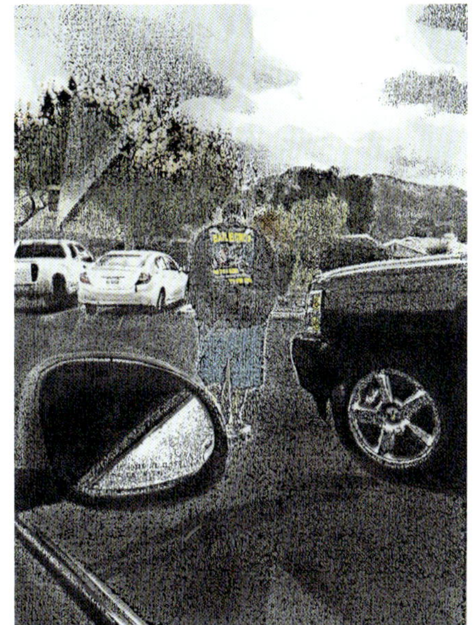

18

19

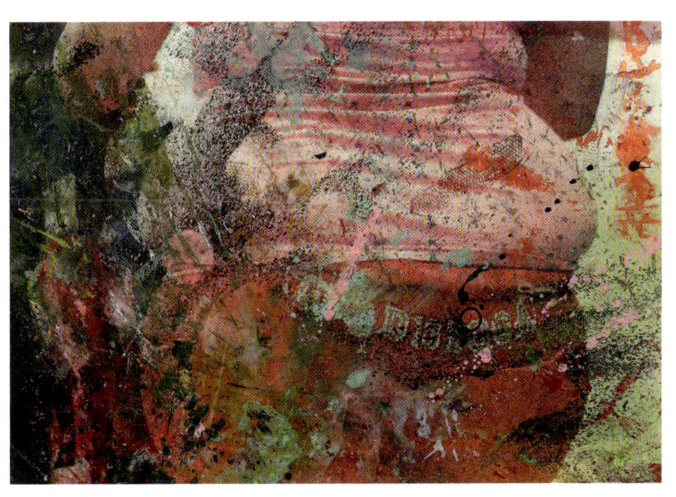

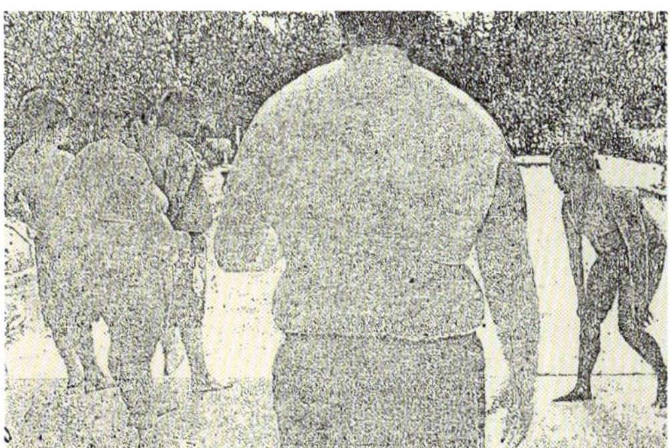

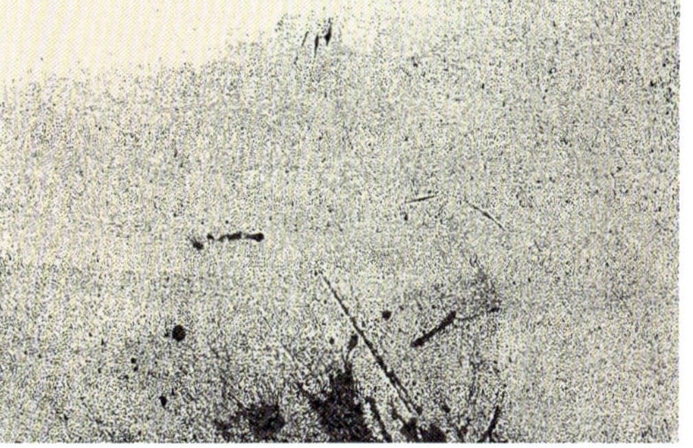

20

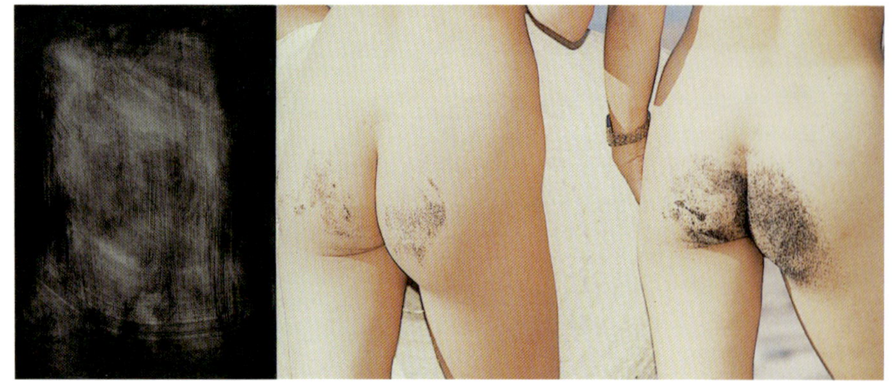

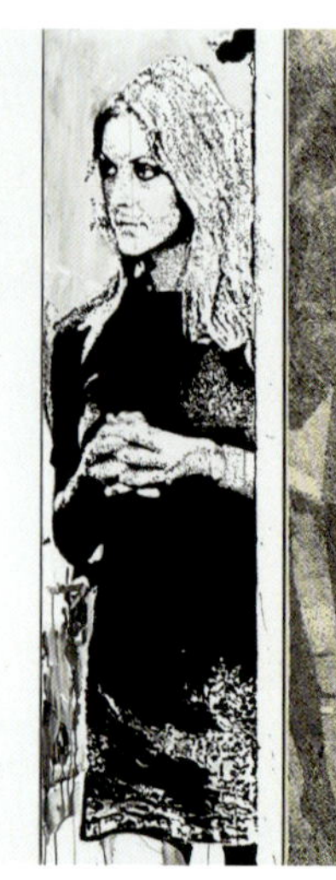
He's running on a treadmill in front of the mirror in his gym. She's coming back from work behind the wheel of her Smart car. Will they meet?

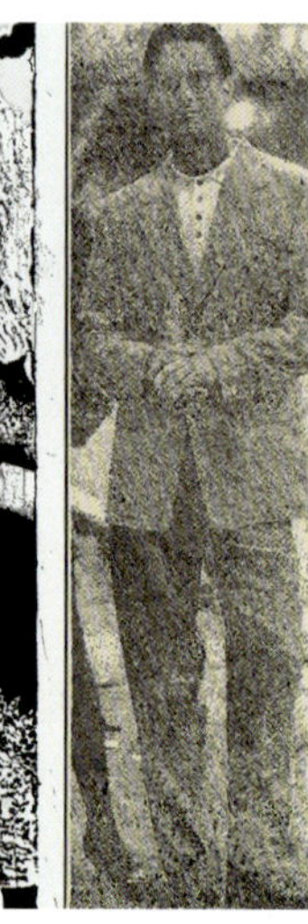

21

22

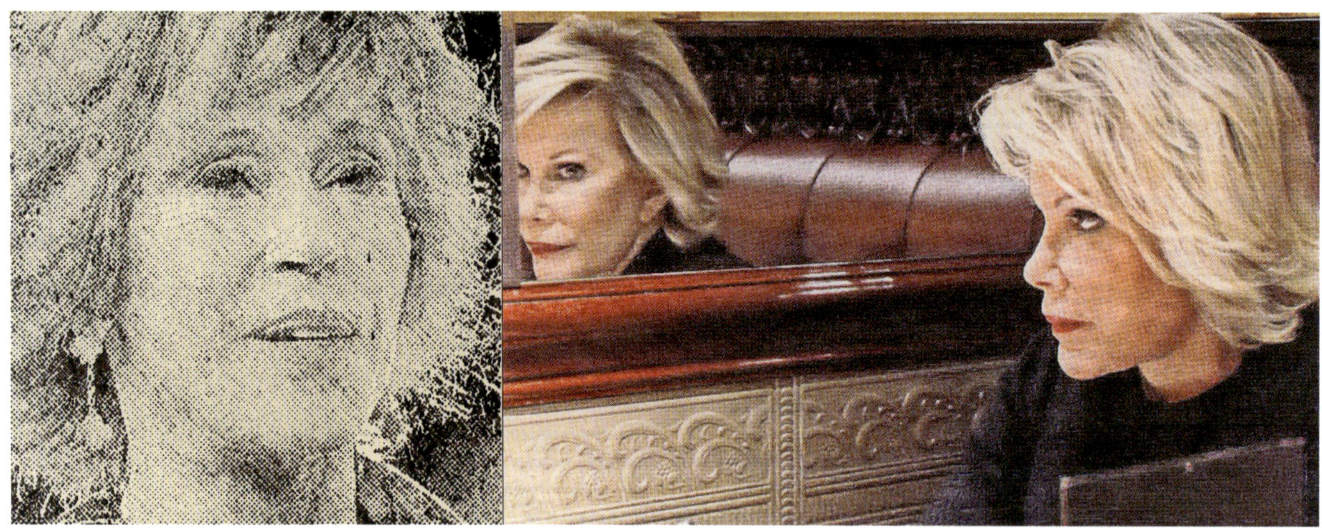

23

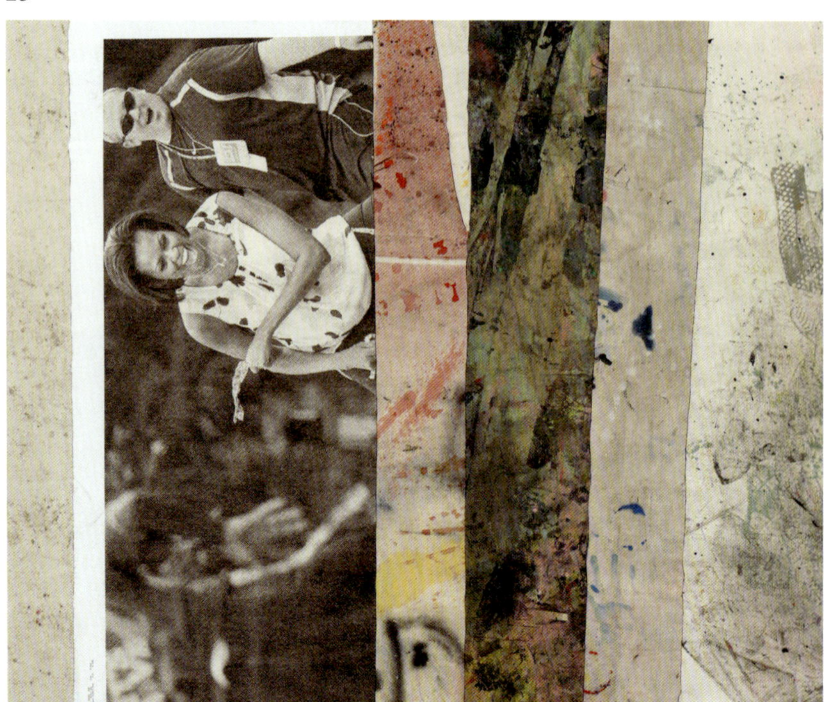

24

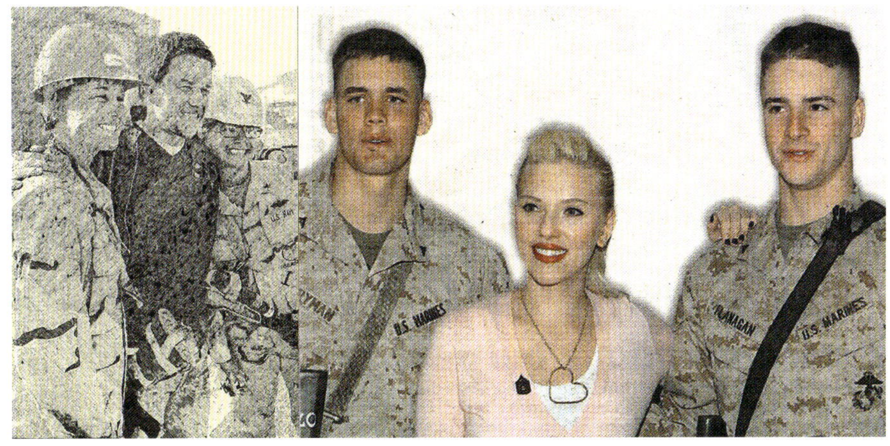
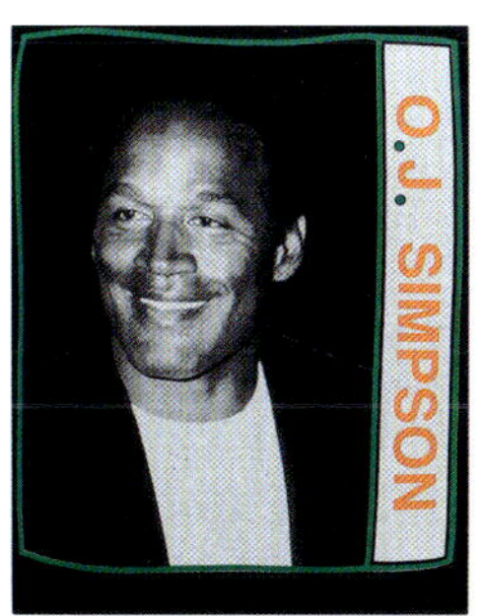
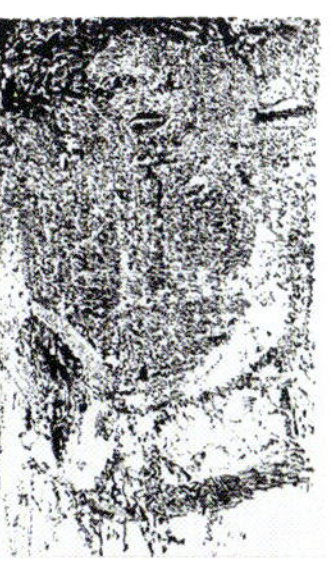

25

26

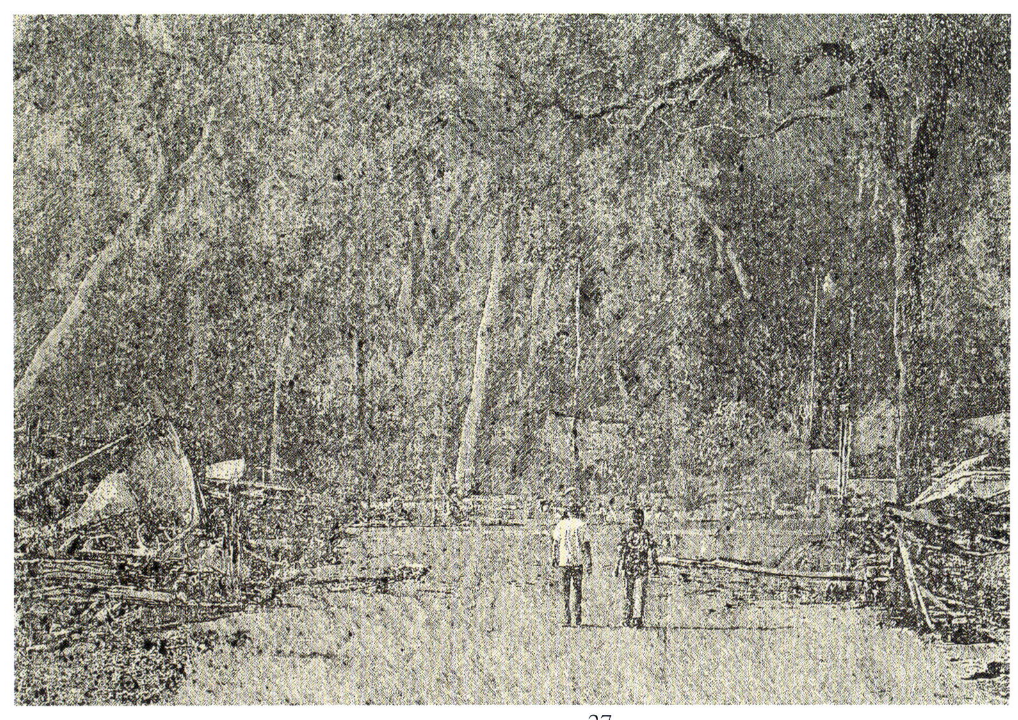

27

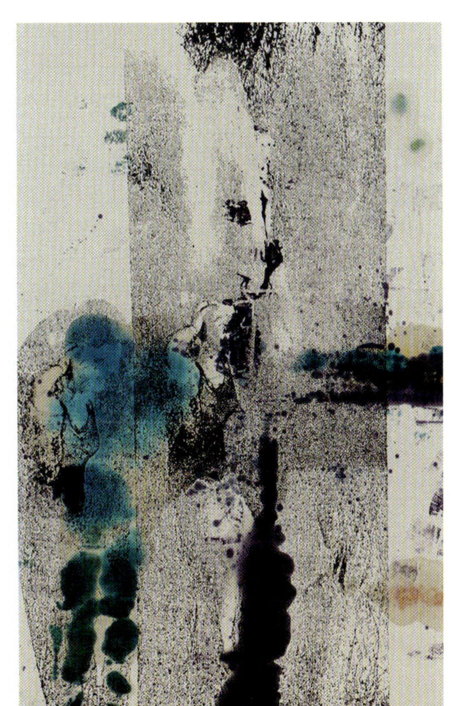
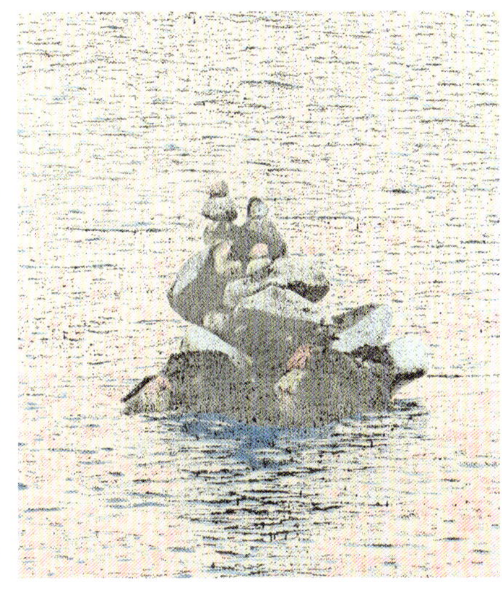
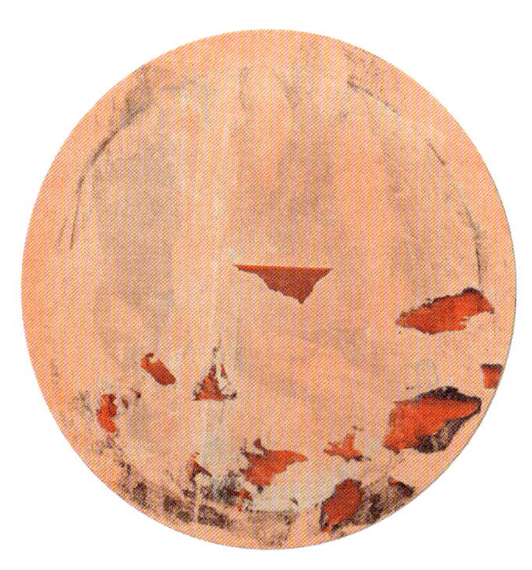

28

29

30

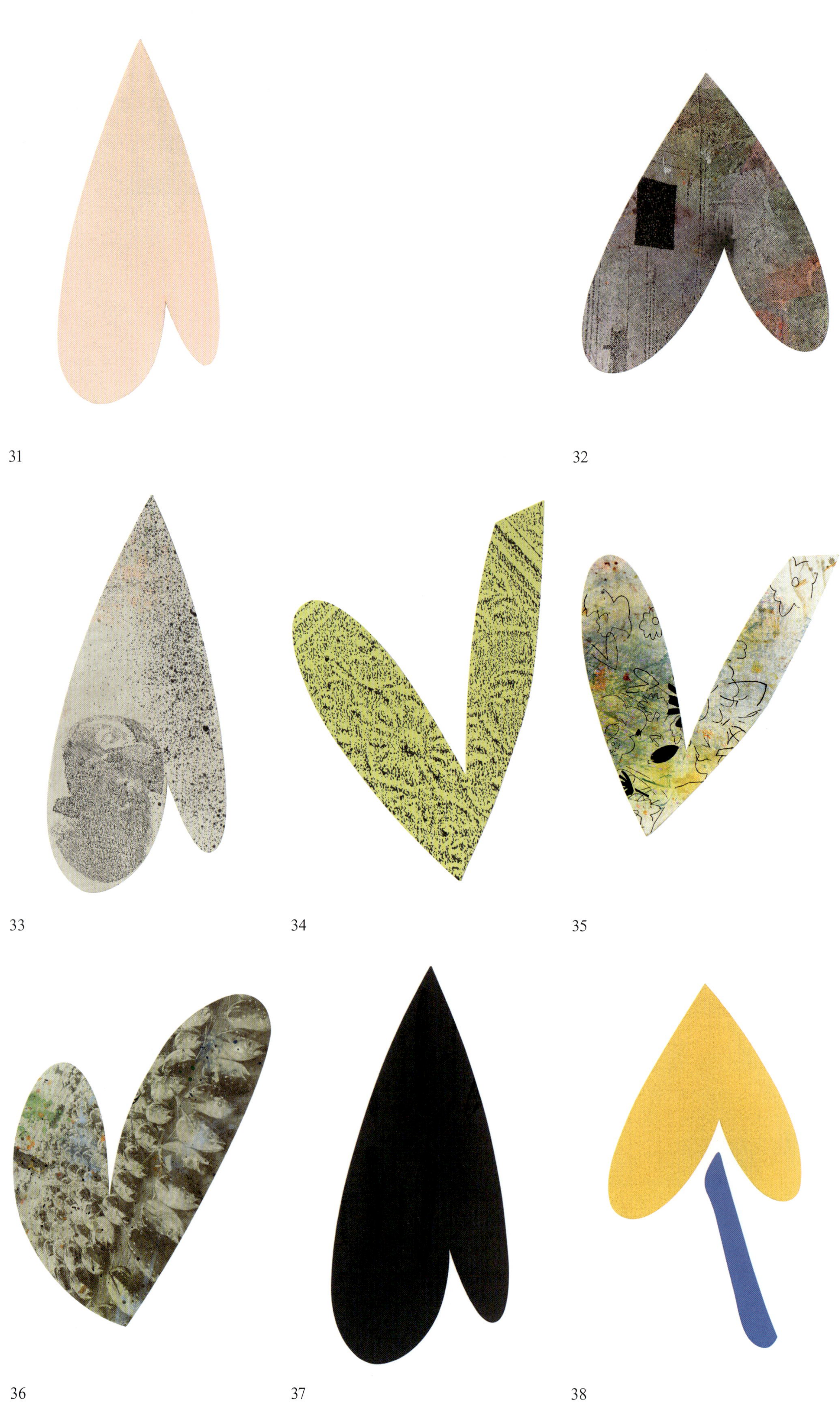

31 32

33 34 35

36 37 38

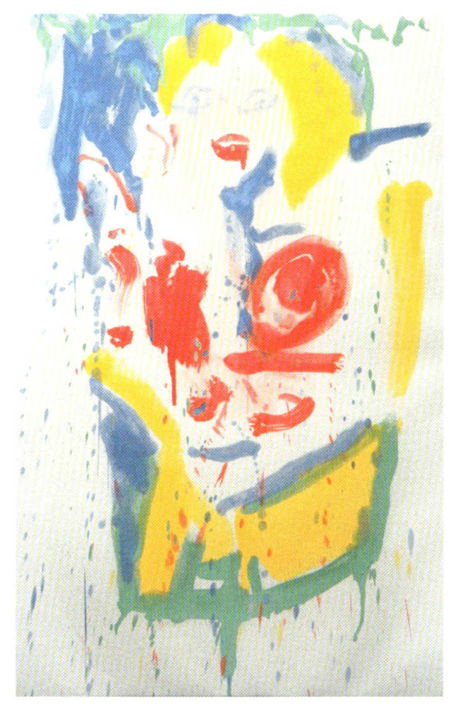

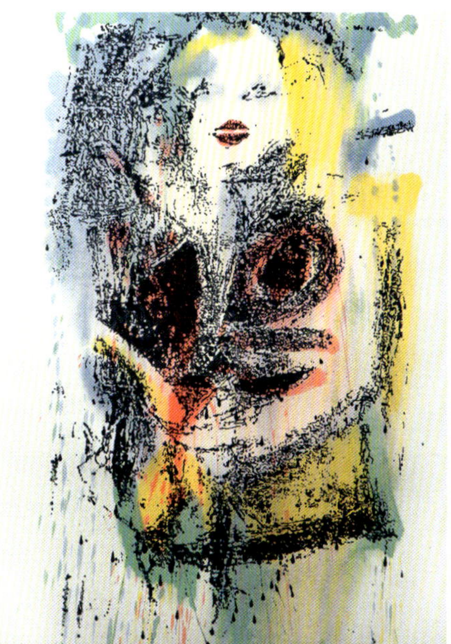

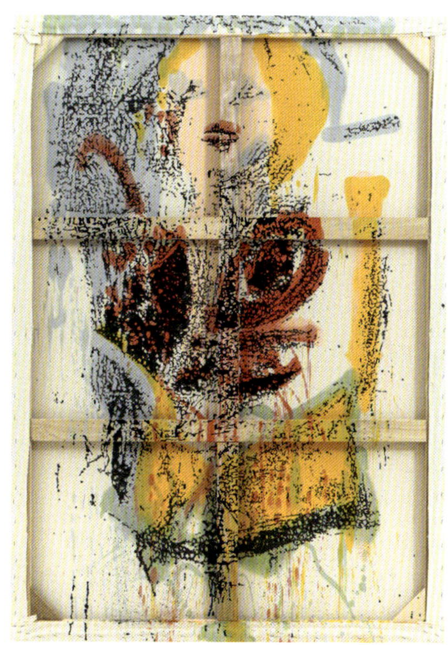

39

40

41

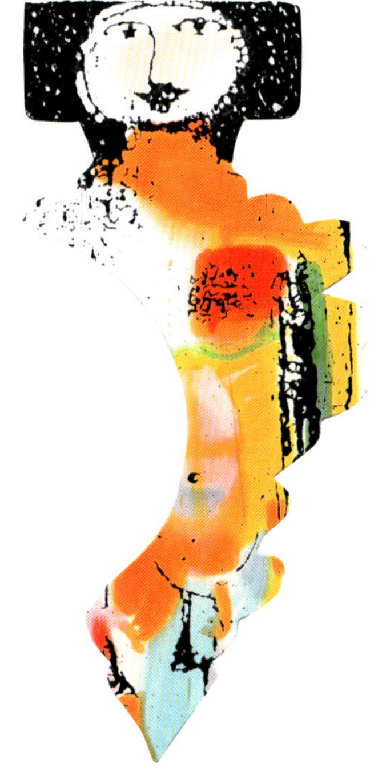

42

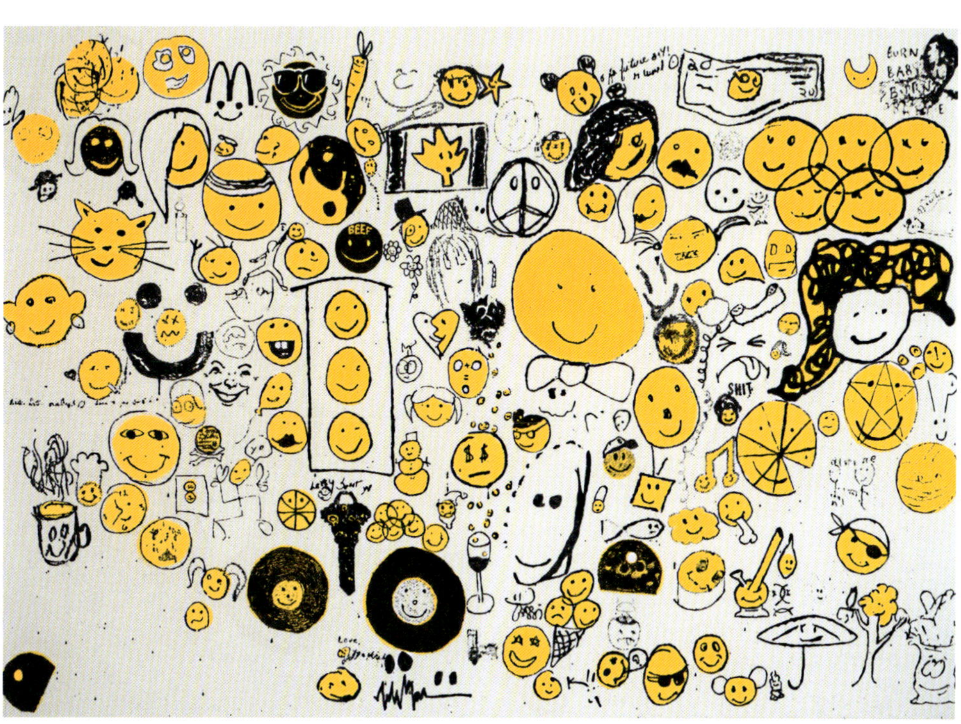

43

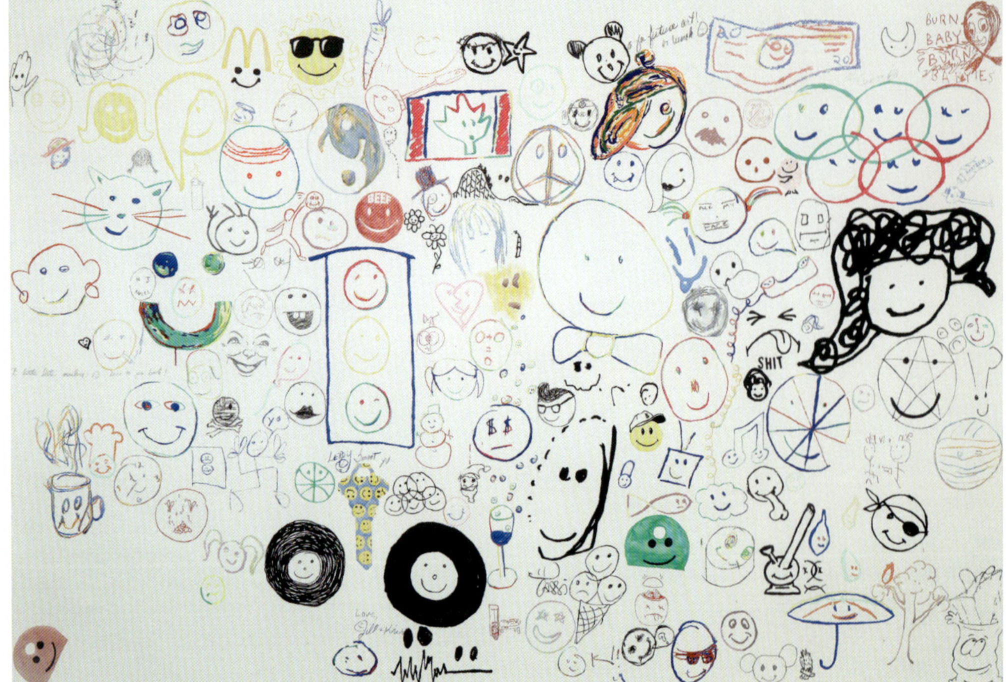

44

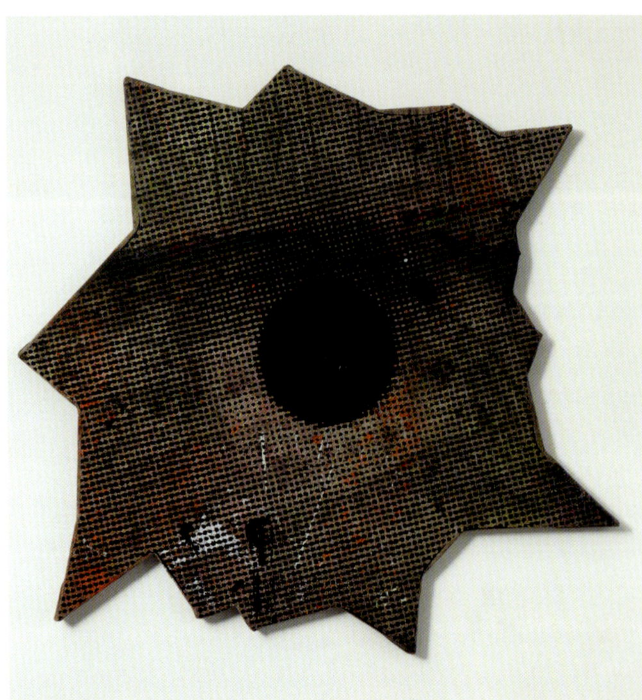

45

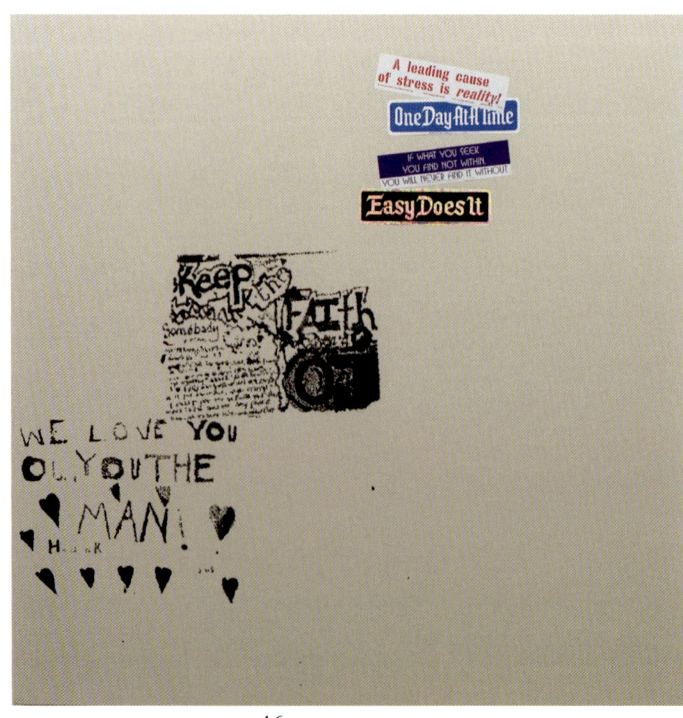
A leading cause
of stress is reality!
One Day At A Time
IF WHAT YOU SEEK
YOU FIND NOT WITHIN
YOU WILL NEVER FIND IT WITHOUT
Easy Does It
Keep the Faith
WE LOVE YOU
O L YOU THE
MAN!

46

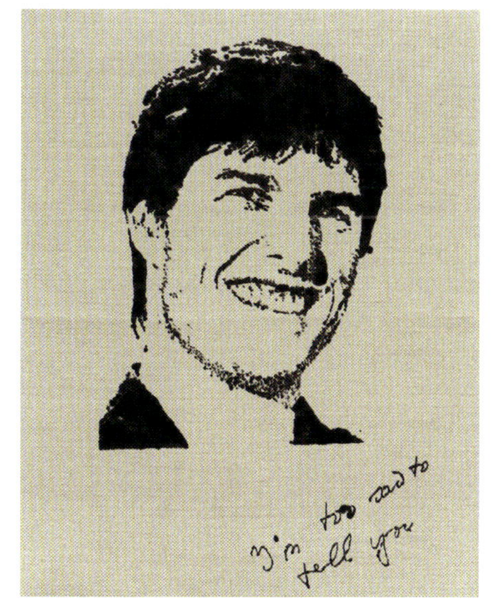

47

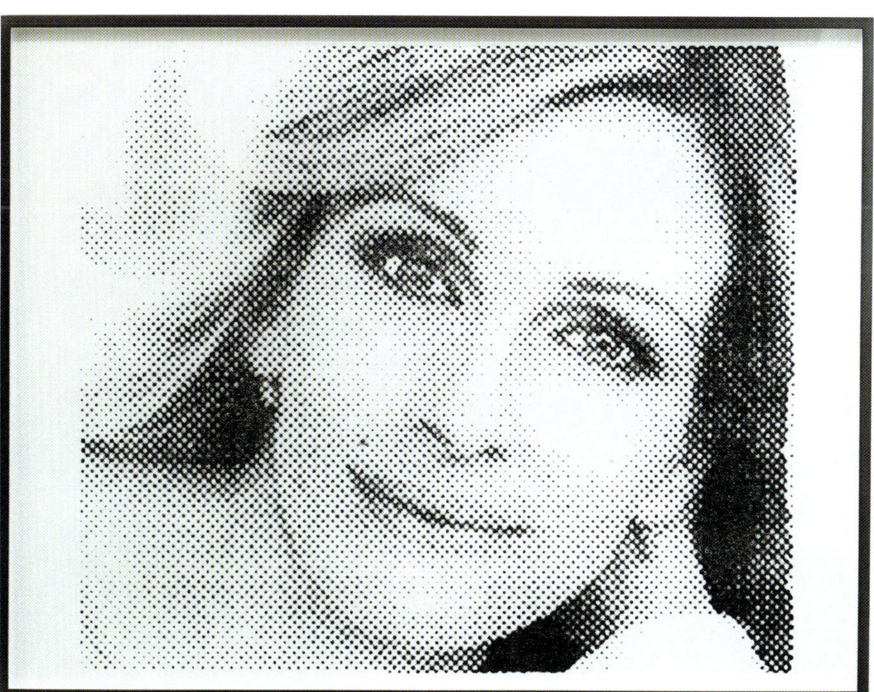

48

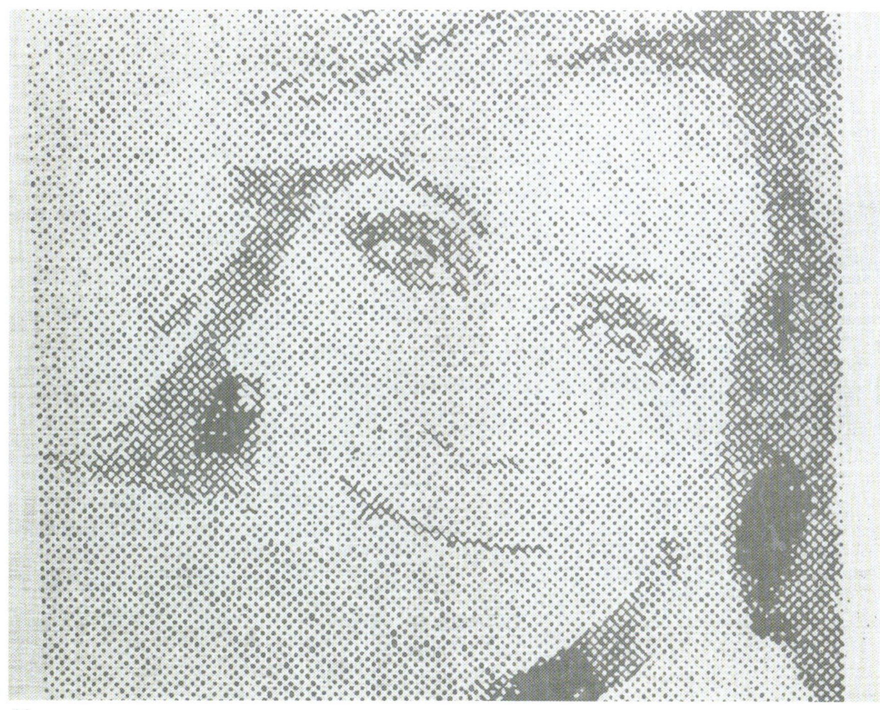

49

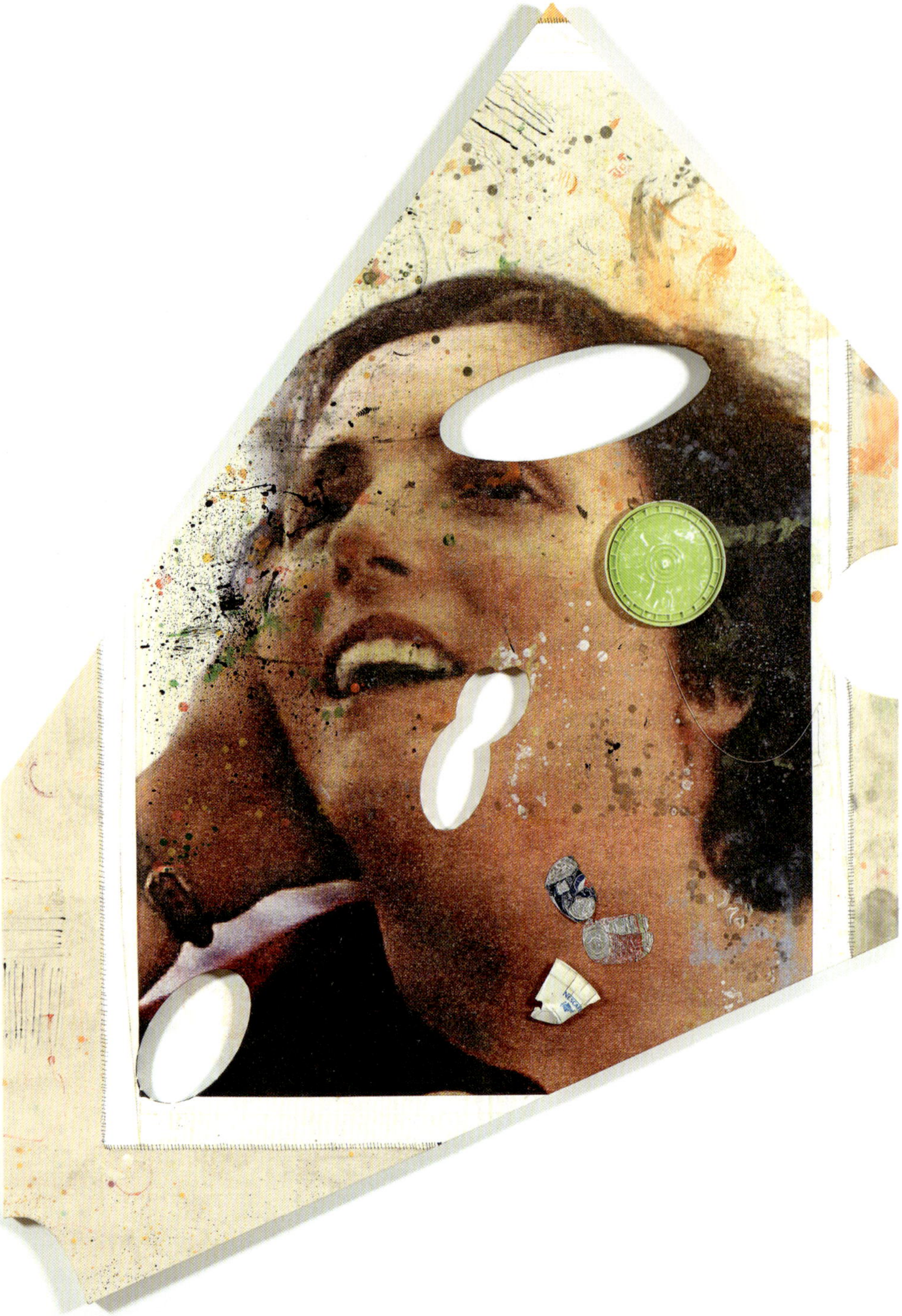

50

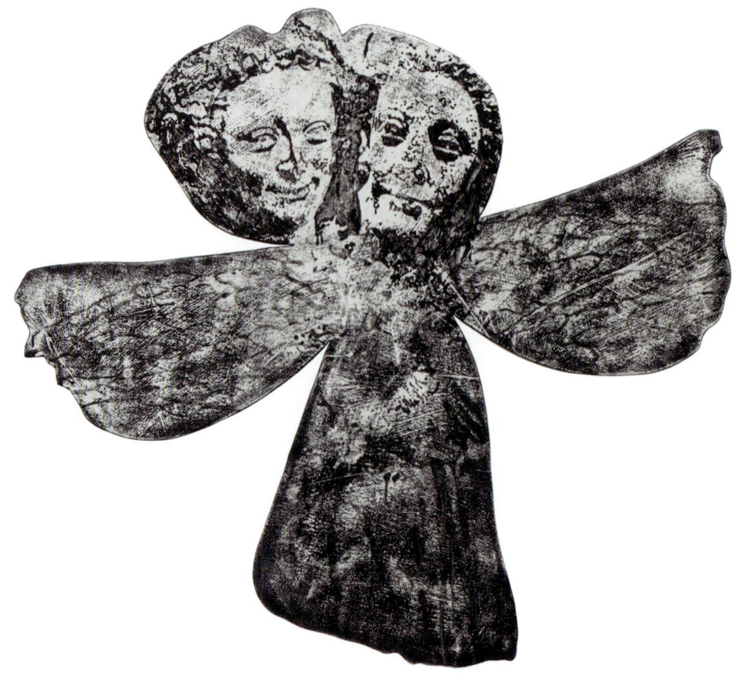

51

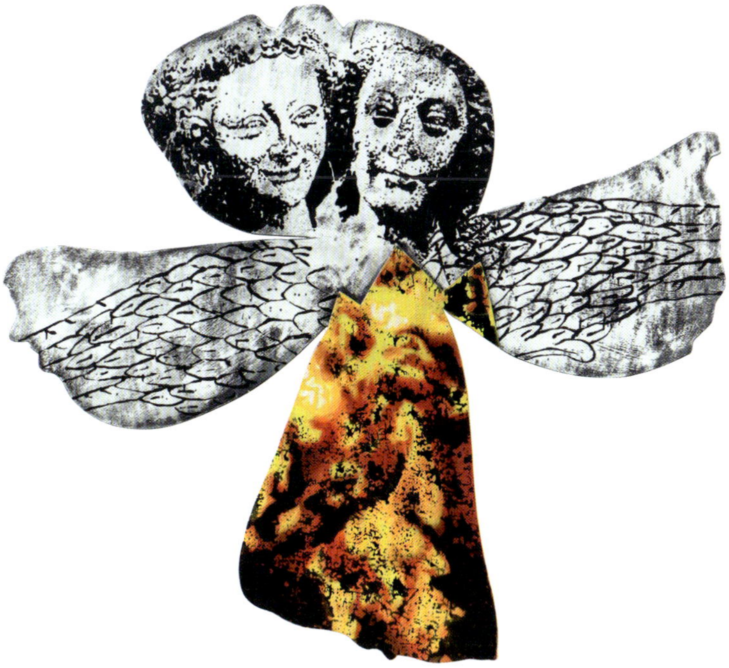

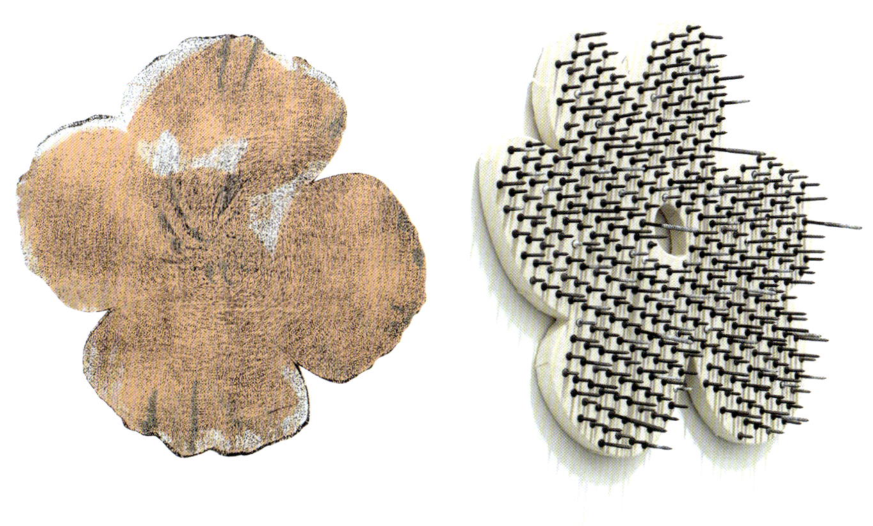

52

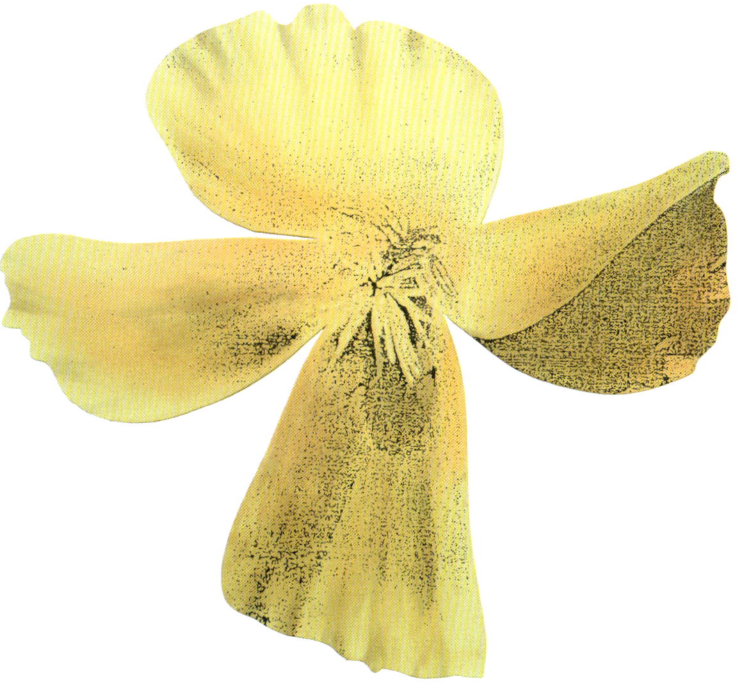

53

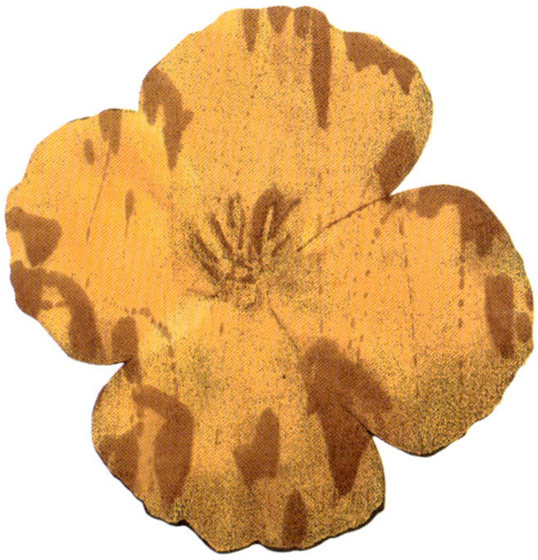

54

55

56

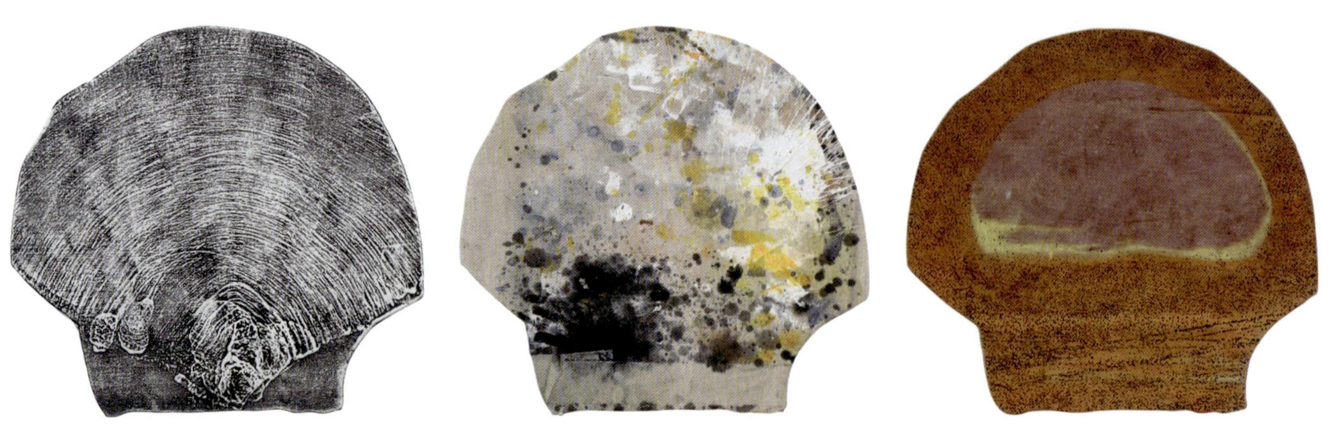

57   58   59

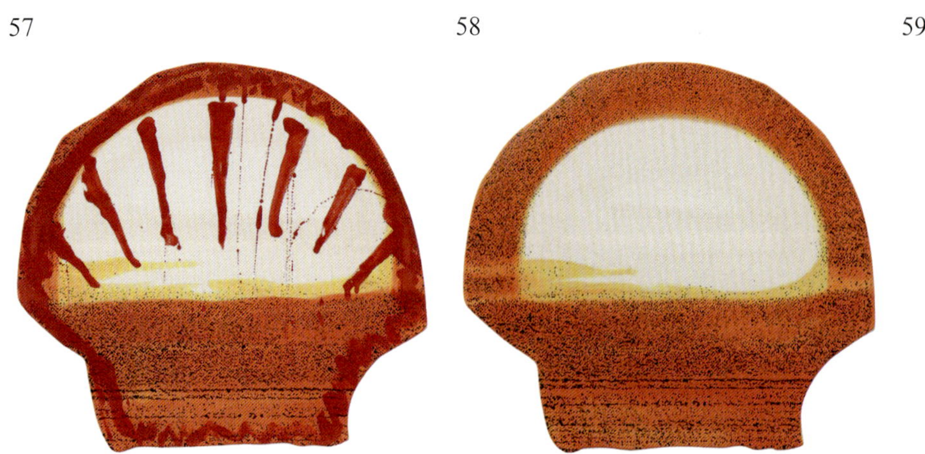

60   61

1   *Before and After*   2014
Oil, alkyd, resin, tape, paper, and dirt on
inkjet on canvas
36 x 150 x 1 1/2 in (91.4 x 381 x 3.8 cm)
Courtesy the artist and Maccarone, New
York/Los Angeles

2   *Before and After Again*   2017
Oil, alkyd, latex, and dirt on canvas
36 x 150 x 1 1/2 in (91.4 x 381 x 3.81 cm)
Courtesy the artist

3   *Ciao Bella #1*   2012
Acrylic and latex on canvas
64 x 45 in (162.6 x 114.3 cm)
Courtesy the artist

4   *M.I.L.F.*   2012 [inside cover]
Alkyd on canvas
84 x 57 in (213.4 x 144.8 cm)
Courtesy Jeanne Greenberg Rohatyn

5   *Orange and Blue Venus With
Stitches*   2017
Oil and dental floss on canvas
37 x 19 x 1 1/4 in (94 x 48.3 x 3.2 cm)
Courtesy the artist

6   *Nicole*   2011
Alkyd on canvas
36 x 28 x 1 1/2 in (91.4 x 71.1 x 3.8 cm)
Courtesy the artist

7   *My Marilyn*   2011
Oil and alkyd on canvas
72 x 33 in (182.9 x 83.8 cm)
Private collection

8   *Marilynstein*   2012 [p. 15]
Oil and alkyd on linen
52 x 72 in (133.1 x 182.9 cm)
Massimo De Carlo, Milan/London/Hong
Kong

9   *Bikinicide #2*   2012
Oil and alkyd on linen
79 x 60 in (200.7 x 152.4 cm)
Rubell Family Collection, Miami

10   *You Make Me (For Christopher
Wool)*   2012
Oil and alkyd on linen
60 x 43 in (152.4 x 109.2 cm)
Collection of David Simkins

11   *Love In The Streets*   2012
Alkyd on linen
36 x 24 in (91.4 x 61 cm)
Private collection

12   *Pimpin Ain't Easy But Somebody
Gotta Do It*   2009 [p. 57]
Alkyd on canvas
48 x 60 in (121.9 x 152.4 cm)
Private collection

13   *Comeback Kate?*   2010
Oil and alkyd on canvas
12 x 18 in (30.5 x 45.7 cm)
Collection of Leo Fitzpatrick

14   *Ghost Town*   2011 [p. 71]
Alkyd on canvas
36 1/4 x 57 1/4 in (92.1 x 145.4 cm)
Collection of Sascha S. Bauer

15   *It's Nothing Personal (Curtains)*
2007
Acrylic on canvas
60 x 72 in (152.4 x 182.9 cm)
Collection of Larry Gagosian

16   *Curtains #2*   2007 [p. 16]
Alkyd on canvas
16 x 20 in (40.6 x 50.8 cm)
Collection of Mark Fletcher and Tobias
Meyer

17   *Give 'em the Finger*   2005 [p. 72]
Latex and airbrushing ink on canvas
20 in (50.8 cm)
Courtesy David Zwirner, New York/
London/Hong Kong

18   *Rear End*   2017
Oil and alkyd on linen
68 1/2 x 54 x 1 1/2 in (174 x 137.2 x 3.8 cm)
Courtesy the artist

19   *Bail Bonds, Temecula*   2016
Oil and alkyd on linen
72 x 54 x 1 1/2 in (182.9 x 137.2 x 3.8 cm)
Courtesy the artist and Maccarone, New
York/Los Angeles

20   *Gold Digga Triptych*   2012–14
Oil, dirt, inkjet, acrylic, and alkyd on
canvas
53 3/4 x 79 3/4 x 1 1/2 in (136.5 x 202.6 x
3.8 cm); 39 x 60 x 1 1/2 in (99.1 x 152.4 x
3.8 cm); 39 x 60 x 1 1/2 in (99.1 x 152.4 x
3.8 cm)
The Ganek Family Foundation

21   *Beach Bums*   2009
Inkjet print and alkyd on canvas (diptych)
25 x 59 in (63.5 x 149.9 cm)
Mugrabi Collection

22   *Will They Meet?*   2011
Latex and alkyd on canvas
Three panels: 74 x 22 in (188 x 55.9 cm)
each
Overall dimensions variable
Private collection

23   *Untitled (Survivor Series)*   2011
Alkyd and inkjet on canvas
Alkyd: 42 x 42 in (106.7 x 106.7 cm);
Inkjet: 42 1/4 x 69 1/2 in (107.3 x 176.5 cm)
Rubell Family Collection, Miami

24   *The Dance*   2012
Oil, mixed pigments, dirt, inkjet print,
spray paint, and dental floss on canvas
66 x 54 in (167.6 x 137.2 cm)
Courtesy the Brant Foundation,
Greenwich, CT

25   *Say Cheese (Survivor Series)*   2011
Alkyd and inkjet print on canvas
Canvas: 42 x 29 in (106.7 x 73.7 cm);
Inkjet: 42 x 59 3/4 in (106.7 x 151.8 cm)
Collection of Mark Fletcher and Tobias
Meyer

26   *Anger Management Diptych (Juice
and DeKooning's Marilyn)*   2005
T-shirt stretched on wooden support; latex
on canvas
20 x 16 in (50.8 x 40.6 cm); 18 x 12 in
(45.7 x 30.5 cm)
Courtesy the artist

27   *Fire (Temecula)*   2011 [p. 2]
Alkyd on canvas
42 x 63 in (106.7 x 160 cm)
The Dicke Collection

28   *Bathing Tourist*   2013
Oil and alkyd on linen
98 x 62 in (248.9 x 157.5 cm)
Courtesy Cromwell Art, LLC

29   *Wisconsin Cairn (Lake Flannery)*
2013
Oil and alkyd on canvas
81 x 74 x 1 1/2 in (205.7 x 188 x 3.8 cm)
Collection of Susan and Leonard
Feinstein

30   *Red Nicole*   2004
Ink and paper on canvas
16 in (40.64 cm)
Courtesy the artist

31   *Pink Heart*   2014
Oil on canvas
40 x 19 x 1 1/4 in (101.6 x 48.3 x 3.2 cm)
Collection of Sascha S. Bauer

32   *Interior Heart Painting (Matisse)*
2015
Acrylic and latex on canvas
48 x 41 x 1 1/4 in (121.9 x 104.1 x 3.2 cm)
Courtesy the artist

33   *Sean Price Heart*   2015
Oil and alkyd on canvas
40 x 19 x 1 1/4 in (101.6 x 48.3 x 3.2 cm)
Courtesy the artist

34   *Yellow Ceiling Heart*   2015
Oil and alkyd on canvas
30 x 27 x 1 1/2 in (76.2 x 68.6 x 3.8 cm)
Courtesy the artist

35   *Nate's Small Heart* 2014
Acrylic and latex on canvas
27 x 38 x 1 1/2 in (68.6 x 96.5 x 3.8 cm)
Courtesy Monica and Richard Weinberg

36   *[Tuna Heart]* 2014
Oil, dirt, alkyd, and inkjet on canvas
49 x 74 x 1 in (124.5 x 188 x 2.5 cm)
Courtesy Jeanne Greenberg Rohatyn and
Jackie Greenberg

37   *Rejects Heart* 2015
Oil and alkyd on canvas
40 x 19 x 1 1/4 in (101.6 x 48.3 x 3.2 cm)
Courtesy the artist

38   *Caps and Stems* 2014
Oil on canvas
76 3/8 x 40 1/2 x 1 1/2 in (194 x 102.9 x
3.8 cm)
Private collection

39   *Nate's Marilyn* 2010
Oil on canvas
36 x 24 in (91.4 x 61 cm)
Courtesy the artist

40   *Nate's Marilyn* 2010
Oil and alkyd on canvas
40 x 30 in (101.6 x 76.2 cm)
Courtesy the artist

41   *Reverse Marilyn* 2012
Oil and alkyd on canvas and wooden
stretcher bars
72 x 52 in (182.9 x 132.1 cm)
Courtesy the Brant Foundation,
Greenwich, CT

42   *Bodyguard* 2014 [p. 1]
Oil and alkyd on canvas
54 x 26 x 1 1/4 in (137.2 x 66 x 3.2 cm)
Courtesy Massimo De Carlo, Milan/
London/Hong Kong

43   *Lonely Hearts Club* 2010
Alkyd and oil on canvas
84 x 125 in (213.4 x 317.5 cm)
Courtesy Jeanne Greenberg Rohatyn

44   *Lump Sum* 2009
Ink and latex on canvas
84 x 125 1/2 in (213.4 x 318.8 cm)
Courtesy David Zwirner, New York/
London/Hong Kong

45   *Nate's Dropcloth Maxima* 2010
Latex and silkscreen ink on canvas
29 1/2 x 32 1/2 in (74.9 x 82.5 cm)
Courtesy the Brant Foundation,
Greenwich, CT

46   *Keep the Faith* 2005
Alkyd and bumper stickers on canvas
60 x 60 in (152.4 x 152.4 cm)
Courtesy David Zwirner, New York/
London/Hong Kong

47   *I'm Too Sad To Tell You* 2006
Alkyd on linen
20 x 16 in (50.8 x 40.6 cm)
Courtesy Mark Fletcher and Tobias Meyer

48   *Thirty Million Dollar Smile
Unreversed* 2012
Screen print
32 x 40 in (76.2 x 101.6 cm)
Courtesy the artist

49   *Grey Julia* 2012
Alkyd on linen
28 x 36 x 1 in (71.1 x 91.4 x 2.5 cm)
Courtesy the artist

50   *This Is Not Not A Painting* 2013
[p. 58]
Inkjet, dental floss, plastic paint bucket
lid, oil, plastic cup, aluminum cans, alkyd,
and dirt on canvas
92 x 77 1/2 in (233.7 x 197 cm)
Courtesy the artist and Maccarone, New
York/Los Angeles

51   *First Untitled Angel Painting* 2017
Latex on canvas
33 x 36 x 1 1/4 in (83.8 x 91.4 x 3.2 cm)
Courtesy the artist

52   *"And The Angels Are Singing But
Their Skirts Are On Fire" for E.S. 2* 2017
Latex, oil, and alkyd on canvas
49 x 60 x 1 1/4 in (124.5 x 152.4 x 3.2 cm)
Courtesy the artist and Maccarone, New
York/Los Angeles

53   *Angel Poppy* 2016
Oil and alkyd on canvas
49 x 60 x 1 1/4 in (124.5 x 152.4 x 3.2 cm)
Courtesy the artist and Maccarone, New
York/Los Angeles

54   *Desiree Set Us Free* 2016
Oil and alkyd on canvas
60 x 60 x 1 1/4 in (152.4 x 152.4 x 3.2 cm)
Courtesy the artist

55   *Spinning Away Into So Many
Nipples (For D.B.)* 2017
Latex on linen
60 x 60 x 1 1/4 in (152.4 x 152.4 x 3.2 cm)
Courtesy the artist

56   *Screw Flower* 2017
Screws on canvas
20 x 16 1/2 x 1 1/4 in (50.8 x 41.9 x 3.2 cm)
Courtesy the artist

57   *Where's The Beach?* 2017
Latex on canvas
17 x 19 x 1 1/4 in (43.2 x 48.3 x 3.2 cm)
Courtesy the artist

58   *Margin Merger Border
Murder* 2017
Alkyd, ink, and latex on linen
17 x 19 x 1 1/4 in (43.2 x 48.3 x 3.2 cm)
Courtesy the artist

59   *Dark Shell/Sunny Side Up* 2017
Oil and alkyd on canvas
17 x 19 x 1 1/4 in (43.2 x 48.2 x 3.2 cm)
Courtesy the artist

60   *Sunset Hell* 2017
Oil, alkyd, and enamel on canvas
17 x 19 x 1 1/4 in (43.2 x 48.3 x 3.2 cm)
Courtesy the artist

61   *Sunset Shell* 2017
Oil and alkyd on canvas
17 x 19 x 1 1/4 in (43.2 x 48.3 x 3.2 cm)
Courtesy the artist

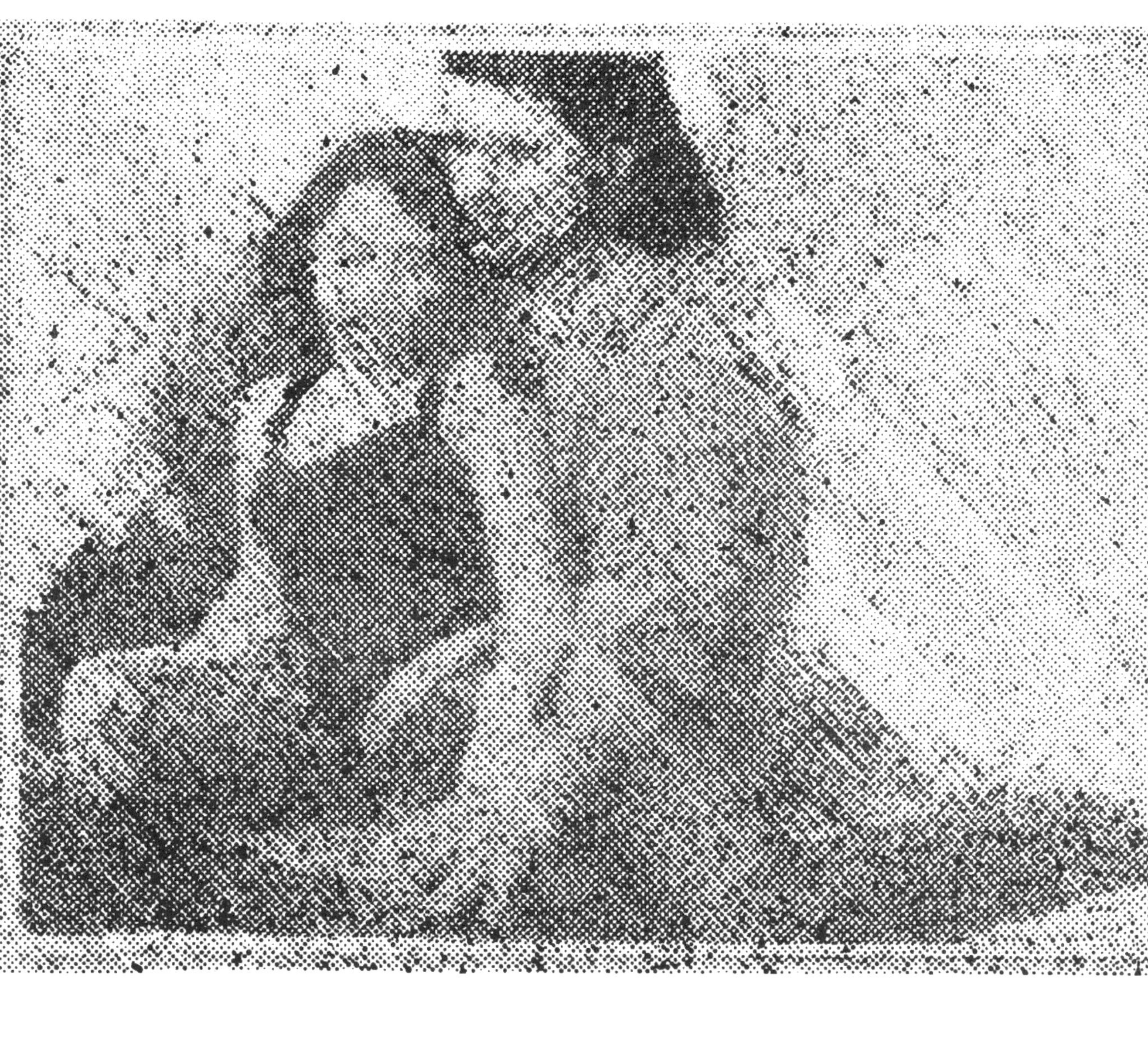

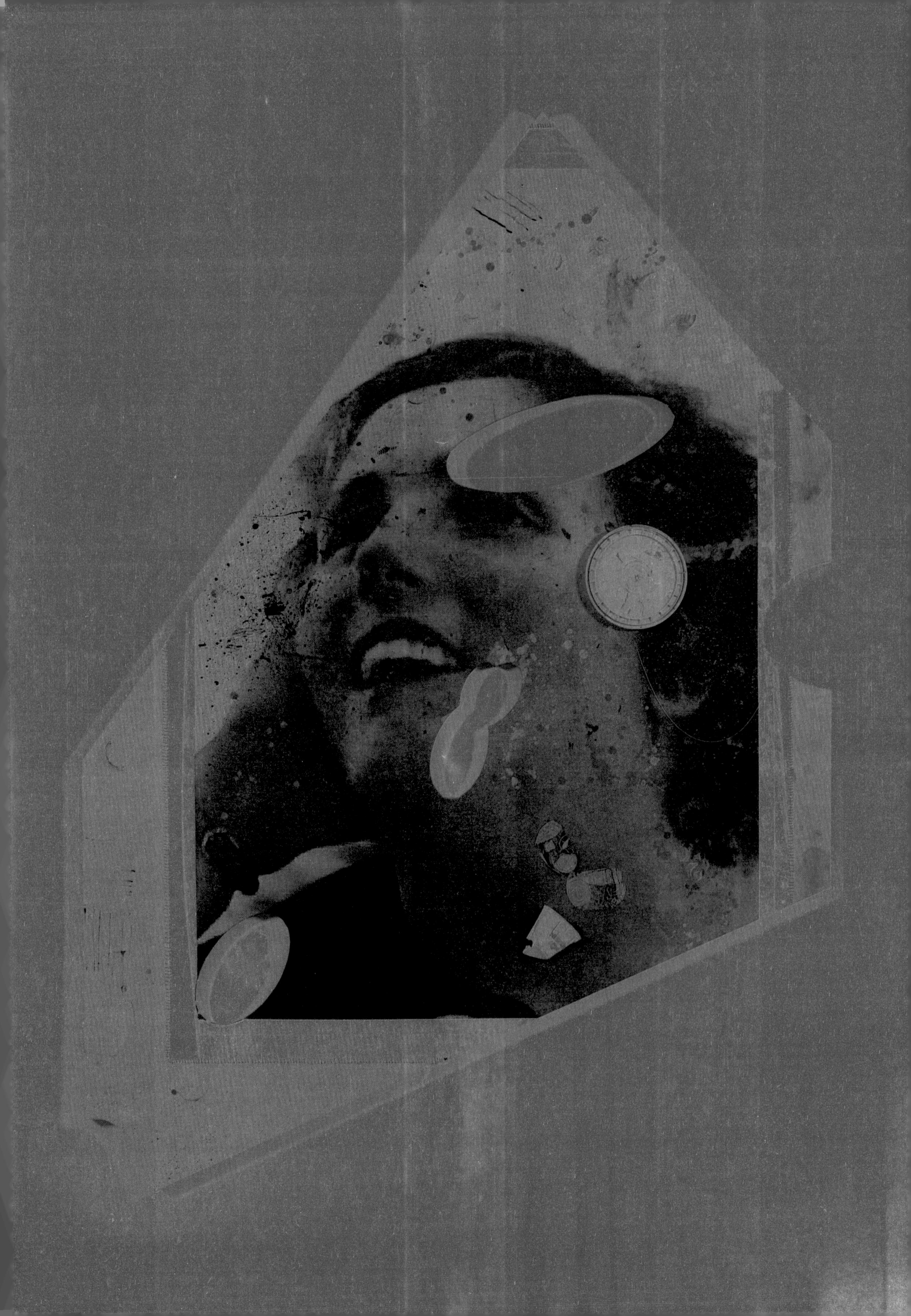

Solo & Two-Person Museum Exhibitions

2018
Nate Lowman: Works from the Astrup Fearnley Collection, Astrup Fearnley Museum of Modern Art, Oslo

2017
Before and After, Aspen Art Museum, CO

2016
World of Interiors, FRAC Champagne-Ardenne, Reims, France

2015
America Sneezes, Dallas Contemporary, TX

2012
The Triumph Arch, with Hanna Liden, 5 Rue de Tilsitt, Paris
I Wanted To Be An Artist But All I Got Was This Lousy Career, Brant Foundation Art Study Center, Greenwich, CT

2011
Three Amigos: Gift Ghost GAP, the American Academy, Rome

2009
The Natriot Act, Astrup Fearnley Museum of Modern Art, Oslo
Nate Lowman, Hydra Workshop, Greece

2006
Axis of Praxis, Midway Contemporary Art, Minneapolis, MN

Group Museum Exhibitions

2015
The Now Forever, Basilica Hudson, NY
Storylines: Contemporary Art at the Guggenheim, Solomon R. Guggenheim Museum, New York
Second Chances, Aspen Art Museum, CO

2014
Empire of Light, Peggy Guggenheim Collection, Venice
Three Blind Mice, with Dan Colen & Rob Pruitt, Museum Dhondt-Dhaenens, Belgium

2013
12th Lyon Biennial, France
Painting in Place, Los Angeles Nomadic Division (LAND), Farmers & Merchants Bank, Los Angeles
Empire State: New York Art Now, Palazzo Delle Esposizioni, Rome
DSM-V, The Future Moynihan Station, New York

2012
Alone Together, Rubell Family Collection, Miami
To Be With Art is All We Ask, Astrup Fearnley Museum of Modern Art, Oslo
We the People, Robert Rauschenberg Foundation Project Space, New York
Holy Crap!, the Fireplace Project, Springs, NY
Do Your Thing, White Columns, New York
(O)IKEA, Hydra Schools Project, Greece

2011
New York Minute, Garage Museum of Contemporary Art, Moscow
George Herms: Xenophilia (Love of the Unknown), Museum of Contemporary Art, Los Angeles
The Luminous Interval: The D. Daskalopoulos Collection, Guggenheim Bilbao, Spain
In the Name of the Artists: American Contemporary Art from the Astrup Fearnley Collection, São Paulo Biennial, Brazil
Karma, White Flag Projects, St. Louis, MO

2010
The Last Newspaper, New Museum, New York
FRESH HELL, Palais de Tokyo, Paris
Off the Wall Part 1: Thirty Performative Actions, Whitney Museum of American Art, New York
A.D.D. Attention Deficit Disorder, Palazzo Lucarini Contemporary, Trevi, Italy
Haunted: Contemporary Photography/ Video/Performance, Solomon R. Guggenheim Museum, New York

2009
Beg, Borrow, Steal, Rubell Family Collection, Miami
Besides, With, Against, and Yet: Abstraction and the Ready-Made Gesture, The Kitchen, New York
New York Minute, MACRO, Rome
When the Mood Strikes: The Cooreman Collection, Museum Dhondt-Dhaenens, Belgium
Mapping the Studio: Artists from the François Pinault Collection, Palazzo Grassi, Venice

2008
Expenditure, Busan Biennial, Korea
Meet Me Around the Corner: Works from the Astrup Fearnley Collection, Astrup Fearnley Museum of Modern Art, Oslo
Unmonumental, New Museum, New York

2007
Memorial to the Iraq War, ICA, London

2006
Defamation of Character, P.S.1 Contemporary Art Center, New York
Down by Law, the Wrong Gallery, Whitney Biennial, New York

2005
Uncertain States of America, Astrup Fearnley Museum of Modern Art, Oslo
Greater New York, P.S.1 Contemporary Art Center, New York

2004
The Mythological Machine, Mead Gallery, Warwick Arts Centre, Coventry, UK
I Love Music, Creative Growth, Oakland, CA

Monographs

Lowman, Nate. *Paintings for Erik*. Eneas Capalbo, ed. Italy: Oratorio Madonna Delle Grazie, Vigoleno, 2019.

Lowman, Nate, and Liden, Hanna. *Cats & Dogs*. New York: Maccarone; London: Massimo De Carlo, London, 2014.

Lowman, Nate, and Lewis, Jim. *Nate Lowman: I Wanted to Be an Artist but All I Got Was This Lousy Career*. Greenwich, CT: Brant Foundation Art Study Center, 2014.

Snow, Dash. *Love Roses*. New York: Karma, 2011.

Lowman, Nate. *Nate Lowman: The Natriot Act*. Oslo: Astrup Fearnley Museum of Modern Art, 2009.

Lowman, Nate. *Nate Lowman: The Hydra Workshops 2009*. London: Sadie Coles HQ, 2009.

Group Exhibition Publications

Rosenthal, Norman, and Gartenfeld, Alex. *Empire State: New York Art Now*. New York: Skira Rizzoli, 2013.

Kvaran, Gunnar B., and Raspail, Thierry. *12th Lyon Biennale – Meanwhile... Suddenly, and Then*. Thomas Boutoux et al., eds. Dijon: Les Presses Du Réel, 2013.

Bellavita, Alessandra. *Disaster / The End of Days*. Paris: Galerie Thaddeus Ropac, 2013.

Bull, Malcolm. *The Show Is Over*. London: Gagosian Gallery, 2013.

Antonitsis, Dimitrios. *(O)IKEA*. Greece: DEMERGON-Daskalopoulos Foundation for Culture and Development, 2012.

Fitzpatrick, Leo. *Not Garbage*. Los Angeles: OHWOW, 2011.

Spector, Nancy, et al. *The Luminous Interval: The D. Daskalopoulos Collection*. New York: Solomon R. Guggenheim Museum Publications, 2011.

Blessing, Jennifer, et al. *Haunted: Contemporary Photography/Video/Performance*. New York: Solomon R. Guggenheim Museum Publications, 2010.

Latitudes, ed. *The Last Newspaper*. New York: New Museum, 2010.

Koh, Terence, et al. *I Want a Little Sugar in My Bowl*. New York: Asia Song Society / OHWOW, 2009.

Gingeras, Alison M., and Bonami, Francesco. *Mapping the Studio: Artists from the François Pinault Collection*. Milan: Electa / Palazzo Grassi, 2009.

Daenen, Ward, et al. *When the Mood Strikes...: Verzameling Wilfried & Yannicke Cooreman*. Belgium: Museum Dhondt-Dhaenens, 2009.

Moos, David, and Zuckerman, Heidi. *Beg, Borrow, and Steal*. Juan Roselione-Valadez, ed. Miami: Rubell Family Collection, 2009.

Phillips, Lisa, et al. *Skin Fruit: Selections from The Dakis Joannou Collection*. Massimiliano Gioni, ed. New York: New Museum, 2010.

Flood, Richard, et al. *Unmonumental: The Object in the 21st Century*. New York: Phaidon Press, 2007.

Kvaran, Gunnar B., et al. *Uncertain States of America: American Art in the 3rd Millenium*. Oslo: Astrup Fearnley Museum of Modern Art, 2005.

Biesenbach, Klaus, ed. *Greater New York 2005*. New York: P.S.1 Contemporary Art Center, 2005.

Contributors

Jim Lewis is the author of three novels as well as numerous catalogues, essays, and articles on art and other matters.

Nate Lowman was born in Las Vegas in 1979. His work has been exhibited at the Museum of Modern Art, New York, the Solomon R. Guggenheim Museum, New York, the Centre Pompidou, Paris, the Whitney Museum of American Art, New York, Palais de Tokyo, Paris, and Palazzo Grassi, Venice. Lowman's work has been the subject of solo exhibitions at Midway Contemporary Art, Minneapolis, Astrup Fearnley Museum of Modern Art, Oslo, Brant Foundation Art Study Center, Greenwich, CT, Dallas Contemporary, FRAC Champagne-Ardenne, Reims, France, and Aspen Art Museum. He lives and works in New York City.

Heidi Zuckerman is the Aspen Art Museum's Nancy and Bob Magoon CEO and Director, overseeing all aspects of the AAM's guiding vision and mission, administrative policies, curatorial and educational practices, strategic planning, and fundraising efforts. She has led the revitalization and re-imagination of the organization, including working with the Board and investors to recast the mission and vision of the museum. Zuckerman's curatorial projects include major solo exhibitions of the work of artists such as Cheryl Donegan, Mark Grotjahn, Gabriel Orozco, Lorna Simpson, and Cathy Wilkes, as well as numerous pivotal group shows. Previously, she served as the Phyllis Wattis MATRIX Curator and then the Chair of the Art Curatorial Department at the University of California, Berkeley Art Museum and Pacific Archive (1999–2005). Prior to this, she served as the Assistant Curator of 20th Century Art at New York's Jewish Museum (1993–98). Zuckerman's writing has appeared in numerous international exhibition catalogues and publications.

Executive
Heidi Zuckerman
Nancy and Bob Magoon CEO
  and Director

Kelsey Nemirov
Executive Assistant

Tyler Schube
Chief Financial Officer

Luis Yllanes
Chief Operating Officer

Curatorial
Jonathan Hagman
Installation Director

Laureta Huit
Registrar

Simone Krug
Curatorial Research Associate

Max Weintraub
Senior Curator

Installation Crew and Art Preparators
Riley Ames
Charlie Childress
John Cohorst
Jason Cook
Vanessa Corona
Takeo Hiromitsu
Natalia Mills
Jason Smith
Dusty Spence
Jed Woolley

Design and Editorial
Monica Davis
Editor

David Wise
Graphic Designer

Development
Charlotte Chesters
Development Assistant

Melissa Jackson
Special Events Director

Simon Klein
Social Media and Marketing
  Assistant

Lexy Mirante
Special Events Coordinator

Abigail Reilly
Development Officer

Education
Annie Henninger
Access and Education Program
  Manager

Elisabeth Strunk
School, Youth, & Family Programs
  Coordinator

Educators
Theresa Booth-Brown
Vanessa Corona
Vanessa Porras
Laci Wright

Finance and Administration
Janelle Caudill
Accounting Clerk

Security and Visitor Information
Zach Carver
Lead Guide

Kathy Marquez
Guide Coordinator

Gregg Yocom
Security Director

Security Officers
Manny Doron
Mark Louderback
Jonathan Mackiwicz
Daniel Martinez

Guides
Lynne Dyson
Ian Edquist
Nikki Hausherr
Rodney Hill
Simon Klein
Erin Malstrom
Susan Martin
Daniel Martinez
Peter Robinson
Raymond Seeman
Sue Shufro
Ines Vergara

Café
Mary Daly
Café Manager

Allen Domingos
Culinary Partner

Julia Domingos
Culinary Partner

Café Service Associates
Emma Chiles
Emmalee Erickson
Heidi Mailloux
Theresa Martine

Building and Facilities
Vince Hart
Facilities Assistant

Shop
Ali McCorkle
Assistant Retail Manager

Shop Associates
Roxy Montoya
Katie Nix

This publication accompanies Nate Lowman's AAM exhibition, *Before and After*, curated by Heidi Zuckerman with Courtenay Finn and Lauren Fulton, and on view in Galleries 2 & 3 at the Aspen Art Museum from December 15, 2017–June 10, 2018.

Published by Aspen Art Press

Aspen Art Museum
637 East Hyman Avenue
Aspen, CO 81611
United States
aspenartmuseum.org

Available through Artbook, LLC

Distributed Art Publishers
155 Sixth Avenue, 2nd Floor
New York, NY 10013
artbook.com

Poster: Courtesy the artist

Photography Credits:
Robert McKeever: 16, 44
Tony Prikryl: 18–32, 41–45, 47, 50–54, 71–72

Library of Congress Control Number:
Names: Lewis, Jim (Writer on art) | Zuckerman, Heidi. | Aspen Art Museum (Aspen, Colo.), organizer, host institution.
Title: Nate Lowman : before and after / Jim J. Lewis, Heidi Zuckerman.
Description: Aspen, CO : Aspen Art Press, 2019. | "This publication accompanies Nate Lowman's AAM exhibition, Before and After, curated by Heidi Zuckerman with Courtenay Finn and Lauren Fulton, and on view in Galleries 2 & 3 at the Aspen Art Museum from December 15, 2017-June 10, 2018." | Includes bibliographical references and index.
Identifiers: LCCN 2019016356 | ISBN 9780934324816 (pbk. : alk. paper)
Subjects: LCSH: Lowman, Nate, 1979---Exhibitions.
Classification: LCC ND237.L815 A4 2019 | DDC 759.13--dc23
LC record available at https://lccn.loc.gov/2019016356
ISBN: 978-0-934324-81-6

AAM exhibitions are made possible by the Marx Exhibition Fund. General exhibition support is provided by the Toby Devan Lewis Visiting Artist Fund. AAM education programs are made possible by the Questrom Education Fund.

Major support for Nate Lowman's *Before and After* was provided by Erin Leider-Pariser and Paul Pariser and Rona and Jeffrey Citrin. Additional support was provided by the AAM National Council.

Nancy and Bob Magoon CEO and Director
Heidi Zuckerman

Curatorial Research Associate
Simone Krug

Chief Operating Officer
Luis Yllanes

Installation Director
Jonathan Hagman

Adjunct Editor
Sarah Stephenson

Graphic Designer
David Wise

Printer
die Keure, Belgium

Typeface
Neue Hass Grotesk
Times Now

Paper
Cover: Splendorlux premium, 180 gsm
Amber graphic, 100 gsm
Novatech matt, 115 gsm
Chromolux 1s coated alu silver, 80 gsm
Poster: 60 gsm Opakaal

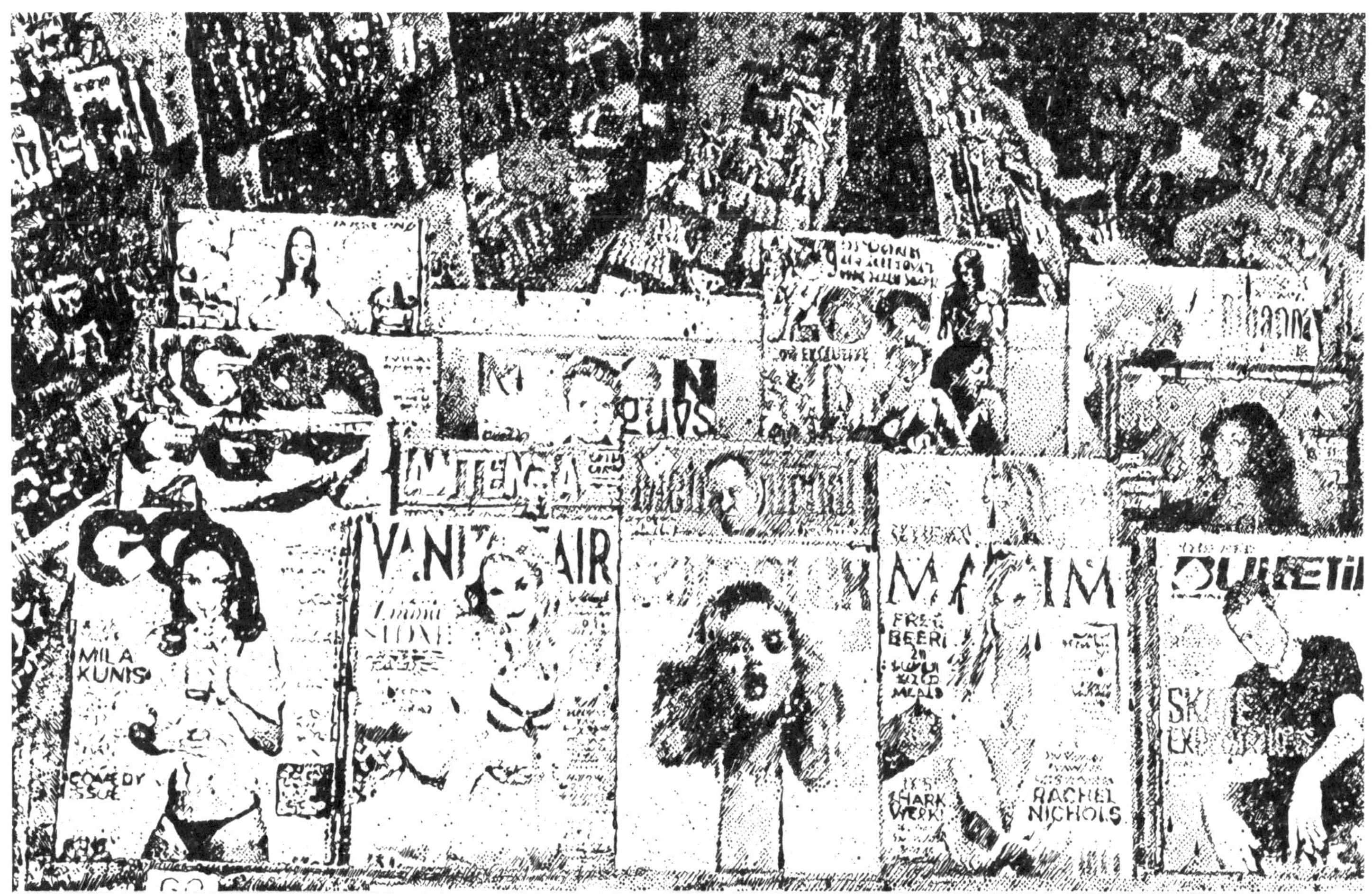

GQ
MILA
KUNIS
COMEDY ISSUE
VANITY FAIR
MAXIM
FREE BEER
IT'S HARD WORK!
RACHEL
NICHOLS

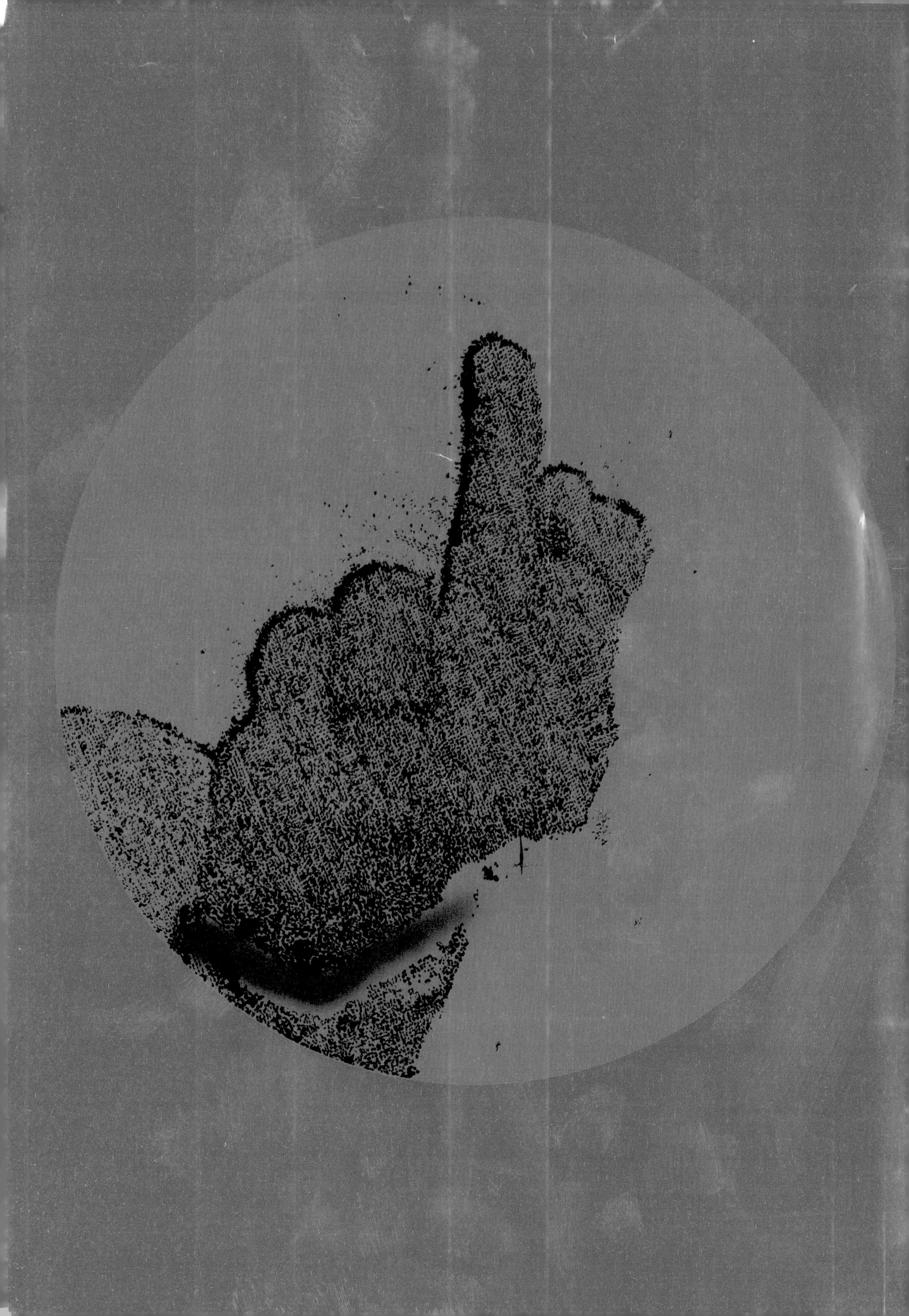